Family Reading Night

Darcy J. Hutchins

Marsha D. Greenfeld

Joyce L. Epstein

EYE ON EDUCATION
6 DEPOT WAY WEST, SUITE 106
LARCHMONT, NY 10538
(914) 833-0551
(914) 833-0761 fax
www.eyeoneducation.com

Library of Congress Cataloging-in-Publication Data

Hutchins, Darcy J.
Family reading night / Darcy J. Hutchins, Marsha D. Greenfeld,
   Joyce L. Epstein.
      p. cm.
   ISBN 978-1-59667-063-1
1. Family literacy programs.
2. Reading--Parent participation.
   I. Hutchins, Darcy J. II. Greenfeld, Marsha D. III. Epstein, Joyce Levy. IV. Title.
   LC149.H88 2007
   372.42'5--dc22

                  2007034492

CREDIT LINE: From AND TO THINK THAT I SAW IT ON MULBERRY STREET by Dr. Seuss, copyright TM &
copyright (c) by Dr. Seuss Enterprises, L.P. 1937, renewed 1965. Used by permission of Random House Children's
Books, a division of Random House, Inc.

CREDIT LINE: From THE CAT IN THE HAT by Dr. Seuss, copyright TM & copyright (c) by Dr. Seuss Enterprises,
L.P. 1957, renewed 1985. Used by permission of Random House Children's Books, a division of Random House, Inc.

CREDIT LINE: From IF I RAN THE ZOO by Dr. Seuss, copyright TM & copyright (c) by Dr. Seuss Enterprises, L.P.
1950, renewed 1978. Used by permission of Random House Children's Books, a division of Random House, Inc.

Book design services provided by Jennifer Osterhouse Graphic Design
3752 Danube Drive, Davidsonville, MD 21035
(410-798-8585)

Also Available from Eye On Education

Building a Culture of Literacy Month-by-Month
Hilarie Davis

Active Literacy Across the Curriculum:
Strategies for Reading, Writing, Speaking, and Listening
Heidi Hayes Jacobs

Literacy from A to Z:
Engaging Students in Reading, Writing, Speaking, & Listening
Barbara R. Blackburn

But I'm Not a Reading Teacher:
Strategies for Literacy Instruction in the Content Areas
Amy Benjamin

Literature Circles That Engage Middle and High School Students
Victor and Marc Moeller

Writing in the Content Areas, 2nd Edition
Amy Benjamin

Writing Put to the Test: Teaching for the High-Stakes Essay
Amy Benjamin

Socratic Seminars and Literature Circles for Middle and High School English
Victor and Marc Moeller

What Great Teachers Do Differently:
14 Things that Matter Most
Todd Whitaker

Seven Simple Secrets: What the Best Teachers Know and Do
Annette Breaux and Todd Whitaker

Classroom Motivation From A to Z:
How to Engage Your Students in Learning
Barbara Blackburn

The National Network of Partnership Schools (NNPS) at Johns Hopkins University invites schools, districts, states, and organizations to join together to use research-based approaches to organize and sustain excellent programs of family and community involvement.

www.partnershipschools.org

Meet the Authors

Darcy J. Hutchins is a Senior Program Facilitator at the National Network of Partnership Schools (NNPS) at Johns Hopkins University. She provides professional development to school, district, and state leaders for partnerships to help them build, evaluate, and sustain comprehensive partnership programs that positively impact student success. Ms. Hutchins was a teacher in the Baltimore City Public School System, where she developed and implemented successful family literacy workshops. She has a Master's of Science degree in Educational Studies from Johns Hopkins University and is completing her PhD in Education Policy at the University of Maryland-College Park.

A Senior Program Facilitator at NNPS, **Marsha D. Greenfeld** provides professional development to help leaders in districts, states, and organizations and school teams to implement and maintain goal-linked programs of family and community involvement. With a master's degree in education, Ms. Greenfeld previously served the Baltimore City Public School System as a classroom teacher and a district Facilitator for School, Family, and Community Partnerships. She also worked in the Technical Assistance Branch of the Office of Federal Grants Programs in Washington D.C. and as a partnership coordinator in the national office of Communities in Schools.

Joyce L. Epstein, Ph.D., is the founder and director of the National Network of Partnership Schools (NNPS) at Johns Hopkins University. For many years, she has conducted research and worked with elementary, middle, and high schools, districts, and state departments of education to develop research-based partnership programs that will improve policy and practice. Dr. Epstein has over 100 publications on the nature and effects of family and community involvement. She serves on numerous editorial boards and advisory panels on parent involvement and school reform. Dr. Epstein is a recipient of the 2005 American Orthopsychiatric Association's Blanche F. Ittleson Award for scholarship and service to strengthen school and family connections.

National Network of Partnership Schools
Johns Hopkins University
3003 N. Charles Street, Suite 200, Baltimore, MD 21218
www.csos.jhu.edu/p2000 • tel: 410-516-8800 • fax: 410-516-8890

Acknowledgments

The authors would like to thank the students, families, and teachers in the Baltimore City Public Schools who participated in our Family Reading Nights. They helped us identify and improve the components that are described in this book.

We would also like to thank members and colleagues of the National Network of Partnership Schools at Johns Hopkins University who have implemented excellent Family Nights and other family and community involvement activities. We are inspired, year after year, by their *Promising Partnership Practices.*

We would also like to acknowledge the reviewers who had read and commented on early versions of the manuscript: Kim Lancaster, Millboro Elementary School, VA; Pat Michael, Ridgefield Public Schools, CT; and Catherine Thome, Lake County Educational Services, IL.

A special thank you goes to our families for their ideas and continual support.

Jennifer Osterhouse, Book Design

Marida Hines, Illustration

Table of Contents

CHAPTER 1

Introduction

What are Family Reading Nights?

Family Reading Nights are events that help parents,[1] students, teachers, and others in the community:

- enjoy reading and literacy activities with their children,
- celebrate students' thinking skills and literacy talents,
- gain ideas for how to help their children at home,
- learn more about the school's reading and literacy curriculum,
- improve students' attitudes about reading, writing, and other literacy skills,
- increase students' literacy skills, and
- recognize the value of teachers working in partnership with families and the community to improve students' opportunities, attitudes, skills, and success in reading, writing, spelling, grammar, and related literacy skills.

Family Reading Nights may be led by teachers, other educators, or parent or community leaders.[2] Typically conducted at school in the evening when most parents can come to school, they also can be conducted during the school day, on weekends, and in locations outside of school.

The exciting news is that there are many formats for Family Reading Nights that may be selected to meet specific goals for improving parents' understanding of students' reading and writing activities, students' attitudes and achievement in reading, and educators' connections with families and the community. This chapter provides an overview of how to organize and conduct successful Family Reading Nights. Chapters 2 through 11 provide details on ten themes for Family Reading Nights that may be conducted throughout the school year. The Appendix includes forms to plan and evaluate Family Reading Nights.

Why conduct Family Reading Nights?

Today, just about all schools set measurable goals in their school improvement plans for student success in reading and literacy. Family Reading Nights contribute to these goals by engaging parents and the community in ways that encourage youngsters to value, share, and enjoy reading, writing, and the other language arts. Family Reading Nights also help schools meet the requirements for family involvement in the No Child Left Behind (NCLB) Act, Section 1118. As one activity in a full program of school, family, and community partnerships, Family Reading Nights help focus involvement on student achievement, as NCLB requires.

Studies of family involvement with students in reading confirm the benefits of parents and children reading at home (Epstein, 2001; Sheldon & Epstein, 2005) and at school (Dearing, Kreider, Simpkins, & Weiss, 2006). The studies show that well-designed and well-implemented subject-specific involvement activities yield positive results for students in reading. Family Reading Nights are one reading-related involvement activity that can involve parents who do not usually participate at school, help them reinforce literacy skills at home, and contribute to students' attitudes and achievement in reading (Darling & Westberg, 2004; Kyle, McIntyre, Miller, & Moore, 2006.)

Many schools struggle to find positive practices to involve families who speak languages other than English at home, who are unfamiliar with schools and the curriculum, who are employed during the school day, or who are otherwise "hard to reach." Family Reading Nights are one way to build positive relationships between and among educators and parents and enable all families to contribute to students' success in school. Indeed, Family Reading Nights are being implemented in schools across the country that serve families who are economically, culturally, and linguistically diverse (Maushard, et al., 2007).

When schools strengthen parents' knowledge of and interest in the reading and language arts curricula, more students learn that their families think reading, writing, spelling, grammar, speaking, and listening are important skills to master. By engaging community partners in reading activities, students learn that other adults enjoy reading and sharing stories. In the elementary grades, students enjoy participating in Family Reading Nights. Students' positive attitudes may improve their desire to learn, increase success in class, and raise test scores.

Of course, the best way to increase students' reading and literacy achievement is to have high-quality instruction by every teacher for every student at every grade level. Family involvement, including well-designed Family Reading Nights, supports excellent teaching and provides extra, out-of-school time for students to practice and sharpen their reading skills. With high-quality teaching *and* family support, Family Reading Nights can help more students achieve the literacy goals in any School Improvement Plan.

Who should be on the Planning Committee?

Planning Family Reading Nights is a team effort, incorporating ideas from teachers, parents, students, and others in the community. A planning committee is led by a chair or co-chairs to oversee the events and ensure that plans are well implemented. One teacher from each grade level or from clustered grades (e.g., PreK-K, 1-3, 4-6) may serve on the planning committee. The school librarian or media specialist has information about school and community resources and funding that could add to the success of Family Reading Nights. Also, it is recommended that at least two parents with students in different grade levels and from different communities (or one parent from each grade level) serve on the planning committee for Family Reading Nights. Helpful community partners (e.g., public librarian, bookstore manager, newspaper columnist, sports figure) also could be on the planning committee or engaged in particular events. Because there are multiple stakeholders in improving children's education, these partners should help plan Family Reading Nights.

The planning committee can be a subgroup of an Action Team for Partnerships, which works together to plan and implement a comprehensive program of family and community involvement (Epstein, et al., 2002).[3] In a full program, a written plan for partnerships includes activities for many types of involvement that are linked to reading and other school improvement goals. It is important for a team of educators, parents, and community partners—not one individual—to plan, implement, and evaluate Family Reading Nights and all family and community involvement activities.

How should Family Reading Nights be designed?

Schools may conduct one or more Family Reading Nights each year. The events must be designed and tailored to support school goals and to meet the needs of the families and students in specific schools.

Consequently, there are many innovative formats for Family Reading Nights. For example, if the planning committee wanted to celebrate students' work, a Family Reading Night could display students' reading and writing projects and have students present or perform their literacy skills. The students might showcase their work in a Writing Café or Poetry Slam, which may coincide with a school Book Fair to increase the number of families and community members who attend.

If the goal for a Family Reading Night were to inform parents about the school's language arts curriculum, state standards, and grade-level benchmarks, the evening would take a different form. In this case, parents would attend an information workshop, while their children completed fun-to-do literacy activities with a Teacher-Leader. There also could be time during the evening for parents and children to come together to enjoy a reading activity.

Schools also conduct Family Reading Nights to help parents gain confidence about conducting reading activities with their children at home. On these nights, parents and students rotate through "stations" guided by Teacher-Leaders, complete various literacy tasks, and practice ways to talk and share ideas with each other. The activities, of course, must be appropriate for students' grade and skill levels, culturally relevant for families and children, and fun for all.

Family Reading Nights will take different forms for specific goals and desired results. The planning committee must start with the end in mind, and select a format that supports its objectives.

What are the major components of successful Family Reading Nights?

Specific practices have been shown to encourage families to attend Family Reading Nights.

Dinner. Because Family Reading Nights are usually held in the evening after many parents get home from work, the school could provide dinner for the families who attend. Business partners often are willing to donate dinner for well-planned, goal-oriented events. The planning committee must ensure that there is enough food for all participants who register to attend. They also may try to accommodate food restrictions or allergies. See a sample Invitation and Registration form in the Appendix.

Student Performances. When students perform a song, dance, dramatic reading, poem, debate, or other literacy-linked production, parents are more likely to attend. The planning committee should invite students from different grade levels to present various literacy achievements at a series of Family Reading Nights so that different parents will be interested in attending.

Active Engagement. Few people enjoy sitting on hard chairs listening to someone lecture for one or two hours. Family Reading Nights must actively involve all participants in completing activities, sharing comments, conducting discussions, and celebrating students' successes. More parents will attend if Family Reading Nights are informative *and* enjoyable.

Publicity. It is essential to inform families about an upcoming Family Reading Night in welcoming words and in languages that can be easily understood. Many schools send home attractive flyers, and add scheduled events to the daily announcements to increase excitement among students. The planning committee may identify groups of parents that they want to attract and personally telephone or e-mail those parents, using translators and interpreters, as needed. The local media, including foreign language radio, cable TV, and newspapers, can help publicize Family Reading Nights in public service announcements. When parents receive good information and reminders about an event, they are more likely to attend.

Incentives. Many schools include surprises or prizes to encourage participation at Family Reading Nights. These include raffles and door prizes for parents, free books for students to take home, and "No Homework" passes for students who attend with their families. Offering incentives, especially items linked to students' reading and writing skills, adds spirit and purpose to the evening and shows participants that their attendance is appreciated.

Child Care. If schools expect parents to attend an evening event, it may be necessary to provide child care for families with very young children. If that is true, the planning committee for Family Reading Nights would arrange for and train adult or teen volunteers to watch and work with toddlers of parents who are attending Family Reading Nights with their school-age children. The school should provide age-appropriate books, movies, toys, or games in the child-care room.

What is the agenda for a Family Reading Night?

The Family Reading Nights described in this book are designed for two hours, after most parents come home from work (e.g., 5:30 to 7:30 pm, or 6 to 8 pm). Time is allocated for the following activities.

First hour: Whole Group Activity

                    Student Performance

                    Dinner

Second hour: Small Group/Breakout Sessions

                    Usually separate for students and their families

                    in the primary grades and intermediate grades

There are exceptions to this agenda. In this book, *Reading Olympics Family Night* asks students and families to visit a series of activity stations, rather than separate breakout sessions for different grade levels. That event also includes a closing ceremony that brings the full group together at the end of the evening to reflect the Olympics spirit.

The agenda is flexible. Some schools combine the whole group activity and dinner to accommodate families who arrive at various times. The student performance follows dinner, before the whole group breaks into separate sessions. Schools may shorten or extend the time for Family Reading Nights to meet the needs of parents, students, and teachers.

How can the community contribute to Family Reading Nights?

Community organizations and individuals support Family Reading Nights in a number of ways (Sanders, 2005). The planning committee may:

- Ask local businesses, including restaurants, to donate meals, beverages, paper products, and other items for a well-planned, goal-oriented Family Reading Night.
- Identify groups that will offer raffle items, supplies for planned activities, books for children to take home, and other materials for successful events.
- Ask the librarian from the school or public library to serve as a guest speaker, share books for different age groups, recommend summer reading lists and activities, and assist students and families to obtain library cards.
- Publicize special events at the public library (author nights, book clubs) to encourage families to participate.
- Nurture connections with all community partners. Acknowledge business partners in the publicity for the events and in school news articles after the activities. Send "Thank You" notes, issue certificates of appreciation, and celebrate community partners as school volunteers.

In good partnerships, the school, families, students, and community all benefit.

What challenges may arise in planning a Family Reading Night?

Challenges occur in planning all family and community involvement activities, including Family Reading Nights. The planning committee should consider some common obstacles and ways to prevent them from occurring so that events will run smoothly.

Dedicate time for the planning committee to meet. Finding time for committees to meet can be difficult because teachers, administrators, and parents are busy people. Nevertheless, some committee meetings are necessary to plan, conduct, and evaluate Family Reading Nights. If only one Family Reading Night is planned, there must be enough time (e.g., a month or two) to prepare for the event. If a series is planned, timely meetings that are convenient for all committee members must be scheduled to ensure adequate preparation for each event.

Leadership for specific responsibilities for Family Reading Nights should be distributed so that small groups or subcommittees can meet as needed. The chair or co-chairs of the planning committee must keep everyone up to date on progress made, needed assistance, next steps, and next meetings. Summaries of meetings must be sent to those who cannot attend. (See the Appendix for a Team Planning Guide.)

Avoid critical scheduling conflicts. Schools are busy places, and often it is difficult to arrange the best times and places for Family Reading Nights. The events must not conflict with dates for state tests, sports teams, concerts, drama productions, or other major activities. The planning committee should set dates for Family Reading Nights early in the school year so that other school groups will not schedule conflicting events.

Some schools combine Family Reading Nights with PTA/PTO meetings or with a spring book fair. Others hold Family Reading Nights on a pre-planned schedule (e.g., the first Tuesday of each month, every other month, or quarterly) to help parents plan ahead.

Meet budgetary limits. Funding is a common concern for schools across the country. Family Reading Nights need not be pricey. The planning committee should estimate the cost of one or more Family Reading Nights and identify the sources of funds.

In some schools, a percentage of Title I funds must be used for parental involvement activities, including costs of Family Reading Nights. In many schools, business partners and volunteers help compensate for low budgets. The school's parent organization (PTA or PTO) may elect to co-sponsor the events and provide funds for food or supplies. Some schools ask participants to pay a dollar or small sum per person for dinner. The proceeds from schools' bake sales, book fairs, and other fund-raisers that enlist parents' support could be used to support family involvement activities. Sometimes, grants are available from federal, state, and local funders for well-designed, goal-linked partnership activities including Family Reading Nights.

Communicate in languages families understand. The number of families who speak languages other than English at home is increasing in schools across the nation as families immigrate to the United States. All locations with linguistically diverse families must work with translators and interpreters in planning, publicizing, and conducting the evening activities so that all families feel welcome, regardless of the language spoken at home.

Translators and interpreters may be school district personnel; bilingual parents, community, and high school volunteers; school staff; and others. They can ensure that invitations are sent in families' primary languages and that materials for Family Reading Nights are translated so that all families can participate. At the event, interpreters can help families understand directions, join discussions, and share ideas with other families. Of course, whether in English or other languages, all materials and activities must be clear, understandable, and appropriate for students' skill levels so that all parents and students enjoy their experiences at Family Reading Nights.

Identify volunteers for needed tasks. Family Reading Nights benefit from well-prepared volunteers. The planning committee does not work alone, but enlists others to conduct successful events. In addition to translating materials and serving as interpreters, as noted above, volunteers are needed to greet parents, serve dinner, watch younger children, conduct sessions, supervise game stations, and clean up. Some schools invite parents to volunteer, whereas others ask Girl Scouts or Boy Scouts, high school students, senior citizen groups, school alumni, and other community organizations to help. Often, teachers and staff volunteer to help with activities and tasks.

Before recruiting volunteers, the planning committee needs to be clear about the number of helpers needed, time involved, tasks to perform, and training required so that volunteers will be comfortable about their responsibilities. All volunteers should be recognized and thanked for their contributions.

Attend to the "nitty gritty." If the devil is in the details, the planning committee must make good plans for each Family Reading Night. There are many things to think about.

Registration. The planning committee needs to know how many families and students plan to attend each Family Reading Night.

This information affects decisions and actions concerning the facility, supplies, dinner, Teacher-Leaders for small groups, and volunteers for other tasks. See the Appendix for the sample Invitation and Registration form that explains that dinner will be served to those who register ahead of time. It is a good idea to plan for those who register and for a few more who may come at the last minute.

Space and location. Many people in a room can be very noisy. The whole group activity, dinner, and student presentation should be in a room that is large enough to fit everyone comfortably (e.g., a cafeteria). Breakout sessions could be in separate classrooms to create a small-group environment, reduce noise, and encourage participation.

Typically scheduled at school, Family Reading Nights also can be conducted at the public library, community center, district office, or other locations if the school is not available.

Timing. Family Reading Nights in this book are scheduled for two hours. The planning committee may need or want to shorten or extend the time to ensure that families can participate. It also is necessary to leave time for participants to move between sessions from one location to the next.

Although typically conducted in the evening, Family Reading Nights also can be scheduled during the school day, after school, and on weekends. The time of day and length of event will affect the activities that can be conducted and the parents who are able to attend or not.

Activities. The Family Reading Nights in this book include a wide variety of activities that promote students' skills in reading, listening, writing, public speaking, drawing, and constructing things. The different themes ask students to practice and share with parents important literacy skills in phonics, spelling, oral reading, word recognition, vocabulary, reading comprehension, questioning, creative thinking, note taking, prewriting, writing, and more (National Reading Panel, 2000; Graham & Perin, 2007). The activities ensure that Family Reading Nights are informative for parents, linked to classroom learning, and enjoyable for all participants.[4]

If only one or two Family Reading Nights are held during the school year, the planning committee may mix and match activities from the various themes that are outlined. The committee also may add or substitute other favorite literacy activities that fit a selected theme.

Supplies. There must be ample supplies for students and families to conduct the various activities. The planning committee will decide whether to supply crayons, markers, or both, more or different kinds of paper or tag board, or use other available supplies for the projects that are described. Extra supplies should be on hand in case mistakes are made or more students and families attend than expected.

Samples and examples. The planning committee and Teacher-Leaders could prepare a sample or example for each project (e.g., sample poster, mobile, puzzle, story paper) to show students and families how their activities for Family Reading Night will look. Samples are most effective when they are large and clearly show the steps that participants will take to complete their own projects.

Tone. Family Reading Nights should be convivial and enjoyable for teachers, students, and families, not a test-like environment. Although reading and literacy skills are reinforced in each event, activities can be spirited, noncompetitive, appropriate for students' grade levels and reading skills (including students who are English Language Learners and those with physical and learning disabilities), and—

most importantly—fun to do. Family Reading Nights are not the time for parent-teacher conferences nor for discussing students' academic or behavioral problems. Rather, the evenings are about celebrating students' ideas and enriching literacy skills.

Photos. A Teacher-Leader, member of the planning committee, or other volunteer may take pictures of activities at a Family Reading Night. These can be displayed on a school's Welcoming Wall, in a newsletter, or on a school's Web site.

Evaluations. Families should evaluate their experiences at Family Reading Nights. On exit evaluation forms, they may rate their satisfaction with the activities and give suggestions for improving future events. See a suggested Evaluation form in the Appendix.

Make changes to adapt the suggested components. This book offers many suggestions for conducting successful Family Reading Nights, all of which can be altered as needed. The directions and ideas may be adapted to meet students' and families' needs and interests. Among other changes, the planning committee may select different themes to match the curriculum, reject themes that could raise religious or cultural concerns in that community, revise materials to match available supplies, read different books aloud, add activities to extend the evening, or remove activities to fit a shorter schedule. In several chapters, Web sites are listed for more ideas and resources. These Web sites, identified at publication, may change or close in the future. The planning committee must review and discuss all of the components, select activities or create alternatives, and make decisions to ensure the most productive Family Reading Nights possible.

Include children and parents who cannot attend Family Reading Nights. Although the goal is to have as many families and children as possible attend Family Reading Nights, some families cannot make it on a particular night. Some students may attend with their friends' families, if their own parents are unable to attend. Some schools arrange transportation networks for families who would otherwise be unable to attend.

Schools also can conduct Family Reading *Days* for parents who cannot come to evening meetings. Some schools conduct the same Family Reading event during the day and in the evening so that different groups of families can attend. Others alternate schedules so that one event is in the evening and the next is held during the day.

The planning committee must consider how many families can be accommodated by the available facility and budget. If the facility has a maximum group size, then registration must note that participation is on a first-come, first-served basis.

The planning committee is encouraged to send some "handouts" home to families who cannot come to Family Reading Nights. For example, most of the *Family Pages* in each chapter could be distributed to families who cannot attend, but who request the materials. Some chapters include suggestions for Classroom and Home Connection. These activities follow the themes of Family Reading Nights. They are started in class and completed for homework in order to engage all students and their families in thinking about a reading theme or literacy skill.

Summary

The following chapters guide educators to work with family and community partners to design and conduct successful Family Reading Nights once a month, from September through June. A planning committee for Family Reading Nights may conduct one event or many in any order. The themes and activities selected should meet the school's goals for increasing students' reading and literacy skills and for improving family and community involvement.

Each chapter:
- Identifies a theme, materials needed, targeted skills, a whole-group activity to start the evening, a student presentation, and breakout sessions for primary and intermediate grades.
- Includes information for Teacher-Leaders to conduct the evening's activities and Family Pages for families and students to work together.
- Provides reproducible items for particular activities.
- Suggests follow-up activities that may be used by classroom teachers.

General planning documents (e.g., a Team Planning Guide, Invitation and Registration form, Sign-In Sheet, Homework Passes for students, and Evaluation) are included in the Appendix.

The planning committee should consider all of the goals, purposes, challenges, and solutions discussed above, and develop good plans. Most importantly, make sure to have fun with wonderful Family Reading Nights!

Chapter Notes

1. We use the word "parent" to mean a person who is responsible for raising a child and who is a key contact for a child at school. This refers to parents, grandparents, foster parents, guardians, or other family members who are responsible for children's education and development. We use the word "family" to mean parents and other family members (including siblings) who may attend Family Reading Nights with their elementary school children.

2. Educators are the curriculum leaders at school, but teachers, counselors, principals, other administrators, parent leaders, and community partners may serve as Teacher-Leaders at Family Reading Nights.

3. In schools that are developing comprehensive, goal-oriented programs of school, family, and community partnerships (Epstein, et al., 2002), the Planning Committee for Family Reading Nights is a subcommittee of the whole Action Team for Partnerships (ATP). The full ATP writes annual plans to engage families and the community in ways that improve students' attendance, behavior, and skills in reading, math, science, and other subjects and to create a welcoming climate of partnership. Family Reading Nights are one part of an annual plan for increasing the involvement of all families with students on specific school improvement goals. Visit the Web site of the National Network of Partnership Schools at Johns Hopkins University at www.partnershipschools.org for research-based approaches to develop comprehensive programs of family and community involvement.

4. In addition to the themes in this book, there are other designs for Family Reading Nights in elementary schools. Some events are developed for units of work in language arts, social studies, science, and other subjects. Themes also may focus on students' interests in history or historical fiction; mysteries; folk tales; tall tales; fables; or myths, sports, and other topics.

References

Darling, S. & Westberg, L. (2004). Parent involvement in children's acquisition of reading. *The Reading Teacher, 57,* 774-776.

Dearing, E., Kreider, H., Simpkins, S., & Weiss, H. B. (2006). Family involvement in school and low-income children's literacy performance: Longitudinal associations between and within families. *Journal of Educational Psychology, 98,* 653-664.

Epstein, J. L. (2001). *School, family, and community partnerships: Preparing Educators and Improving Schools.* Boulder, CO: Westview Press.

Epstein, J. L., Sanders, M. G., Simon, B. S., Salinas, K. C., Jansorn, N. R., & Van Voorhis, F. L. (2002). *School, family, and community partnerships: Your handbook for action, second edition.* Thousand Oaks, CA: Corwin Press.

(continued)

Graham, S., & Perin, D. (2007). *Writing next: Effective strategies to improve writing of adolescents in middle and high schools—A report to Carnegie Corporation of New York.* Washington, DC: Alliance for Excellent Education.

Kyle, D. W., McIntyre, E., Miller, K. B., & Moore, G. H. (2006) *Bridging schools and home through family nights: Ready-to-use plans for grades K-8.* Thousand Oaks, CA: Corwin Press.

Maushard, M., et al., eds. (2007). *Promising partnership practices 2007.* Baltimore: Center on School, Family, and Community Partnerships.

National Reading Panel. (2000). *Teaching children to read: An Evidence-Based Assessment of the Scientific Research Literature on Reading and Its Implications for Reading Instruction.* U.S. Department of Health and Human Services (NIH PUB. NO. 00-4769).

Sheldon, S. B. & Epstein, J. L. (2005). School programs of family and community involvement to support children's reading and literacy development across the grades. In J. Flood and P. Anders (eds.), *Literacy Development of Students in Urban Schools: Research and Policy* (pp. 107-138). Newark, DE: International Reading Association (IRA).

Sanders, M. G. (2005). *Building school-community partnerships: Collaboration for student success.* Thousand Oaks, CA: Corwin Press.

CHAPTER 2

Books We Love! Family Reading Night
(September)

Students and families enjoy sharing their favorite books and stories at the *Books We Love! Family Reading Night*—a good theme for the start of a school year. The discussions focus on books students read during the summer, books that parents enjoy reading aloud with their children, or just all-time favorites. Students and parents may bring a favorite book with them to show and share.

Books We Love! Family Reading Night includes a whole group activity that celebrates favorite books, a student presentation that spotlights many kinds of books students love, and activities for the primary and intermediate grades.

We Love It—So Will You!
(Whole Group)

Families will create posters for their favorite stories or books. The posters should entice others to read these favorites. Posters should include the title and author of the book and a big, colorful picture showing something about the story or main character. The posters should be displayed and families may take a "gallery walk" to identify books that they, too, would like to read.

Materials

- 11 x 17 drawing paper or poster board
  (Pre-line paper to show spaces for title, author, and picture.)
- Crayons and/or markers
- Optional collage materials (e.g., colored paper, scissors, glue)
- *Family Page: We Love It—So Will You!*
- Notepaper for gallery walk
- Tape or poster putty to hang posters

Skills Reinforced

- Identifying main idea
- Summarizing

OUR FAVORITE BOOKS (STUDENT PRESENTATION)

Prior to *Books We Love! Family Reading Night,* select one class or grade level to be "poster children" for their favorite books. Teachers will guide them to create posters for display at the event. Students should focus on different kinds of books they love, including fiction and nonfiction, sports stories, histories, biographies, fairy tales, folk tales, adventure stories, mysteries, humorous books, and others. If this is the first Family Reading Night of the year, the posters may feature books that students enjoyed during the summer.

At *Books We Love! Family Reading Night,* display the students' posters with labels of the various genres of favorite books. This will introduce some of the themes of *Family Reading Nights* that will be conducted during the year. A few students (three to five) may give short reports about *why* they enjoy different types of books. Students in the featured class will create a different poster with their families at the event.

We Love It—So Will You!
(Whole Group)

Welcome to *Books We Love! Family Reading Night*. Some books become treasured friends. Tonight, we will make a poster to show and share one of your favorite books with others. Your poster may entice other students and families to read the same book you enjoyed.

Here's what to do.

1. Discuss your favorite books with your family and select one to feature on a poster.

   - Talk together about what was special or enjoyable about the book. Was it one of the characters? Did a strange event or something special happen?

   - Select *one* important character, major event, or important theme to show—in large size—on your poster.

2. Use the art materials on your table to create a poster.

   - Write the title and author in large, neat letters across the top of the paper.

   - Feature one main idea that you love about the book in a big, colorful picture.

3. Each family will sign their poster and hang it along with the others.

4. Take a gallery walk and look at the other posters on display.

   - Ask the family poster-makers about books that interest you.

   - Use notepaper to write down the titles of books that members of your family might like to read.

Hang Out With Your Favorite Story (K-2)

Materials

- Selection of favorite books. Or, invite students to bring one favorite book.
- *Family Page: Elements of a Story*
- *Family Page: Hang Out With Your Favorite Story*
- Wire or plastic hangers (one per family)
- Tagboard cut in various shapes (e.g., six-to-eight-inch circles, triangles, squares, ovals), with one hole punched at the top of each shape (at least three shapes per family)
- String
- Scissors
- Crayons and/or markers
- Sample mobile for display/demonstration

Skills Reinforced

- Conveying main ideas
- Identifying story elements

Activity

1. After welcoming participants, describe one of your favorite easy-to-read children's picture books. For example, informally, tell something you like about a character, setting, mood, and plot of *Whistle for Willie* by Ezra Jack Keats, or *The Very Hungry Caterpillar* by Eric Carle, or another favorite book that children might know.

2. Then, in a more formal way, discuss the common features of all stories with the *Family Page: Elements of a Story*. (This page may be duplicated and distributed or used as a chart for discussion.)

3. Guide students and families to work together to recall a favorite book or story. They may discuss a book they know well, one from the collection in the room, or a book they brought from home.

4. Students and families will use the *Family Page: Hang Out with Your Favorite Story* to plan and make a mobile about their favorite book.

5. Share and discuss the completed mobiles to discuss favorite stories with the whole group.

Hang Out With Your Favorite Story (K-2)

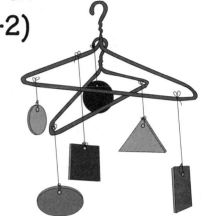

Favorite stories are fun to hear over and over. With your family, create a mobile that shows a few exciting things that happened in one of your favorite stories. We will hang the mobiles and share the stories.

Here's what to do.

1. Think of your favorite story or book. If you brought one from home, you can look through it.

2. Discuss with your family your favorite parts of the story. List a few ideas.

   <u>Setting</u>: Where did the story take place? _____

   <u>Characters</u>: Which character was your favorite? _____

   <u>Plot</u>: What are two to three important or fun things that happened in the story?

   _____

   _____

   _____

   Why did you like this story or book?

   _____

   _____

3. On three shapes for your mobile, draw pictures about the story. Put the title of the story and author (if you know it) on one side of each shape. Then, draw a character, one or two important events that you enjoyed, or the setting on the three shapes.

4. Use strings to hang the shapes on a hanger.

5. Share the story on your mobile with others at your table and with the whole group.

We Are in the Book (3-5)

Materials

- Selection of favorite books. Or, invite students to bring one favorite book.
- *Family Page: Elements of a Story*
- *Family Page:* We *Are in the Book.*
- Writing paper
- Drawing paper
- Pencils
- Crayons and/or markers

Skills Reinforced

- Identifying main ideas
- Writing creatively

Activity

1. After welcoming participants, describe one of your favorite children's books that students may know. For example, tell something that you like about a character or the setting, mood, and plot of *Miss Nelson is Missing* by Harry Allard or *Strega Nona* by Tomie DePaola.

2. Then, in a more formal way, discuss the common features of all stories with the *Family Page: Elements of a Story*. (Note: This page may be duplicated and distributed or used as a chart for discussion).

3. Guide students and families to work together to recall a favorite book or story. They may discuss a well-known book, one from the collection in the room, or a book they brought from home.

4. Students and families will use the *Family Page:* We *Are in the Book* to rewrite one scene or one part of a favorite story to include someone from their family. The family members may become the main characters, minor characters, new characters, or they may enter the story as themselves.

5. Share and discuss the completed stories with the whole group. Enjoy the fun of hearing family names inserted in favorite stories.

We Are in the Book (3-5)

Favorite stories are fun to hear over and over. With your family, think of a book or story that you enjoy. Add one or more of the members of your family as characters in the tale. How do you think the story—or your family member—will change?

Here's what to do.

1. Think of a favorite story or book. If you brought one from home, you can look through it.

2. Describe for your family a scene or section of the story that you like best.

3. Decide with your family: How could you *add one or more members* of your family to the story?

   Which story did you select?_____

   Which family member(s) will you put in the story? _____

   _____

   Where in the story will your family member(s) appear? _____

   _____

   Will your family member(s) (check ☑ one)

   ❑ Replace a character? OR ❑ Act as a new character in the scene?

4. Write or rewrite a scene in the story to include your family. In one or two paragraphs, tell what your family member is doing in the story.

5. Take turns with another family at your table to read the new stories that include your family members. Discuss:

   How did the plot or events of the story change when your family member was added?

Classroom and Home Connection

Teachers may involve all students in a discussion of their favorite books, whether or not they attended *Books We Love! Family Reading Night.*

In the classroom:

1. Create a Book Worm, Book Train, Book Giraffe, or other creation for the classroom wall or bulletin board to show "book segments" that get longer throughout the year.
2. Enable students to talk about their favorite books with other students as they add their recommendations to the growing book creature.

Encourage students to do the following at home:

1. Read for pleasure for at least 20 minutes each night.
2. Discuss the books they read with a family partner.
3. Set up a Library Corner at home for their books. This may be a place to read or talk about books with a member of the family or friends.
4. Set up a Writing Center in their Library Corner. This may be a place to write a journal, stories, or reports about books they read.

Teachers may recommend award-winning books to students.

Winners of the Newbery Award (best children's books in the United States) at http://www.scholastic.com/newbery/

Winners of the Caldecott Award (best picture books in the United States) at http://content.scholastic.com/browse/article.jsp?id=4512

Other books to love on the Web site of Reading Is Fundamental, at http://www.rif.org/educators/books/book_list_index.mspx

Explore the Community

Hang the posters and/or mobiles of favorite books that were made at *Books We Love! Family Reading Night* in a community setting such as a library, senior citizen facility, or local business.

Invite the public librarian to *Books We Love! Family Reading Night* to meet students and families, provide library cards to those who need them, offer book lists on favorite children's books, and answer questions about the library.

Elements of a Story (K-5)

SETTING—The time and location of the story.

Setting includes:

Place—Where does the action of the story take place?

Time—When does the story take place?
(e.g., time of day, year, history)

Mood—What feeling is created?
(e.g., cheerful, frightening, thoughtful)

The setting may change during a story. There may be more than one place, time, weather, and mood in a story.

CHARACTERS

Who are the people in the story?

How do they look and act?

What do they say and do?

What do others say about them?

How do others react to them?

PLOT

The plot has a beginning, middle, and end.

How do events happen in the story?

What main ideas develop?

The story may get complicated, but then problems are solved.

For a more detailed list of story elements visit:
http://hrsbstaff.ednet.ns.ca/engramja/elements.html

CHAPTER 3

Scary Stories Family Night
(October)

Scary stories and poems are exciting for students and families to read together. *Scary Stories Family Night* includes discussions of what makes a story scary and how characters solve scary situations.

This event includes a whole group activity for children and families to talk about scary things, a student creative drama, a primary grades activity based on *Where the Wild Things Are*, and an intermediate grades activity of writing an original poem or story.

A Scary Survey
(Whole Group)

Families will complete *A Scary Survey* and draw a picture of something frightening.

Materials
- *Family Page: A Scary Survey*
- Drawing paper
- Crayons and/or markers

Skills Reinforced
- Identifying main ideas
- Summarizing information

THINGS THAT GO BUMP IN THE NIGHT (STUDENT PRESENTATION)

Prior to *Scary Stories Family Night*, select one class to dramatize a well-known children's scary story, poem, or song. It may be a simple story with a scary section (such as *The Berenstain Bears and the Spooky Old Tree* or the Berenstains' *Bears in the Night*), a short mystery from the school library, or another tale (see ideas from http://www.monroe.lib.in.us/childrens/semiscarybib.html).

The creative drama should be short—no more than 15 minutes. The class should rehearse the presentation at least once before performing it at *Scary Stories Family Night*.

Alternative Student Presentation

Select one class or grade level to draw pictures of the scary part of a story or poem that they read in class. At *Scary Stories Family Night*, display the students' drawings. Include the authors and titles of the stories and the names of the student artists. Ask three to five students to explain their pictures, why the story was scary, and why they enjoyed the story or poem that they illustrated.

A Scary Survey
(Whole Group)

Welcome to *Scary Stories Family Night!* We hope you enjoy the activities.

1. We will start with a family survey to find out what "scares our pants off!" One member of the family will conduct the survey. Another member will answer the questions to tell if something is *not scary, a little* scary, or *very scary* to them.

   Who is asking the questions? _____

   Circle (1), (2), or (3) to show your partner's answers.

   Who is answering? _____

   What scares you and your family the most?

ASK: How Scary is THIS to YOU?	Not Scary	A Little Scary	Very Scary
Dark rooms	(1)	(2)	(3)
Monsters	(1)	(2)	(3)
Snakes	(1)	(2)	(3)
Bugs	(1)	(2)	(3)
Report cards	(1)	(2)	(3)
Bullies	(1)	(2)	(3)
Scary movies	(1)	(2)	(3)
Thunder and lightning	(1)	(2)	(3)
Going to the doctor's office	(1)	(2)	(3)

Discuss with your family:

2. Do you like to read scary stories or see scary movies? Why or why not?

3. What is the scariest story or movie you know? What makes it scary?

4. Everyone in the family may use drawing paper and art supplies to draw something that is scary to them. Write one sentence about the picture at the bottom of the drawing. Explain your picture to your family partner and to others at your table.

Wild and Scary Stories (K-2)

Materials

- Short, scary story to read aloud
- *Where the Wild Things Are* by Maurice Sendak, to read aloud
- Drawing paper
- Crayons, pencils, and markers
- *Family Page: A Wild and Scary Story*

Skills Reinforced

- Sequencing events
- Determining cause and effect

Activity

1. Read one good, short, scary story to the group. This may be *There's a Nightmare In My Closet* by Mercer Mayer, or *There's a Monster Under My Bed* by James Howe, or another favorite story appropriate for the primary grades.

2. Distribute the *Family Page*. Ask the students and families: What did the author do to make the story, poem, or movie scary? See if their ideas match the list on the *Family Page: What Makes a Story Scary?* Discuss other ideas.

3. Introduce the book *Where the Wild Things Are* by Maurice Sendak.*

   a) Tell the group: Here is a famous book about things that scared a little boy named Max. (Note: Do *not* read the book yet.)

   b) Show ONLY the illustrations in the book.

   c) STOP after the three double-paged illustrations of the monsters. (Do *not* show the last few pages when Max returns home.)

4. Tell the students and families to discuss questions they have about the pictures in *Where the Wild Things Are* and what they *think* will happen next.

   Direct the students and families: Use the paper and art supplies to draw a picture showing what you think will happen to Max next. You can draw one picture together or each person may draw an idea of what will happen next.

   After the pictures are completed, ask a few families to share their questions and pictures with the whole group.

5. Read *Where the Wild Things Are* aloud. Tell the group: Listen to see if your questions are answered.

   Discuss: Is the ending the same or different from your drawings of *possible* endings? Did you like the story? Did you think it was scary? Why or why not?

*Teacher-Leader's Resource: The Spanish version of Sendak's *Where the Wild Things Are* is *Donde Viven Los Monstruos*. Translated by Teresa Mlawer. New York: Harper Collins, 1996.

Wild and Scary Stories (K-2)

Do you like to read something scary once in a while? Tonight, we will listen to a scary story and see what authors do to write a frightening tale.

1. Listen to the Teacher-Leader read a short story. Discuss: What did this author do to make the story scary?

   WHAT MAKES A STORY SCARY?

   ■ The story may happen at night or when the character is alone.

   ■ A character thinks there are monsters, ghosts, or other creatures that will frighten or hurt him/her.

   ■ Something happens that a character cannot understand or control.

   ■ A character must do something unusual or extraordinary to get out of a scary situation.

   What else would make a story scary? _____

Where the Wild Things Are by Maurice Sendak

2. Before you hear the story, enjoy the illustrations the Teacher-Leader will show in *Where the Wild Things Are* by Maurice Sendak.

3. Talk with your family:

   What questions do you have about the story and illustrations?

   What would YOU do if you were Max and met these monsters?

4. Draw a picture of what you and your family THINK will happen NEXT.

5. Listen to *Where the Wild Things Are*. After the story is read, discuss:

   Did you guess what happened next or was your idea different from the author's?

   Did you like the story? Did you think it was scary? Why or why not?

There's a Monster in My House! (3-5)

Materials

- Short, scary story to read aloud
- *Family Page: There's a Monster in My House!*
- *Poem: Help! There's a Monster in My Closet*
- Writing paper
- Drawing paper

Skills Reinforced

- Identifying main ideas
- Sequencing ideas

Activity

1. Read one good, short, scary story to the group of students and families. This may be *My Mama Says There Aren't Any Zombies, Ghosts, Vampires, Creatures, Demons, Monsters, Fiends, Goblins, or Things*, by Judith Viorst, or *Harry and the Terrible Whatzit*, by Dick Gackenbach, or another short story that is appropriate for students in grades 3-5.

2. Discuss with the group of students and families: What does an author do to make a story, poem, or movie scary? See if their ideas match the list on the Family Page of *What makes a Story Scary?* Discuss any other ideas.

3. Explain to the group: I am going to read a poem, *Help! There's a Monster in My Closet*. Listen to see if you can tell what the poem is about.

4. Discuss with the group:
   - What do you think this poem is about?
   - What clues did the poet give you about the mystery?
   - What other names could that monster have today? (e.g., Dirt Devil, Oreck).

5. Tell the group: Now, choose an item at home that YOU can turn into "a monster." Don't tell us what your monster is. With your family, write a short story or poem about your monster-thing. Use the list of ideas for making your story or poem scary to write about your object. When your story is done, draw a picture of your monster.

6. Share several stories, poems, and pictures to enjoy the group's imagination. See if others can guess what the monster is in each story or poem before showing the picture.

There's a Monster in My House! (3-5)

Do you like to read something scary once in a while? Tonight we will listen to a scary story and poem, and see what authors do to write a frightening tale. Then, you can try to write one.

1. Listen to the Teacher-Leader read a short story. Discuss: What did this author do to make the story scary?

WHAT MAKES A STORY SCARY?

- The story may happen at night or when the character is alone.

- A character thinks there are monsters, ghosts, or other creatures that will frighten or hurt him/her.

- Something happens that a character cannot understand or control.

- A character must do something unusual or extraordinary to get out of a scary situation.

    What else would make a story scary? _____

    _____

2. Listen to the poem, *Help! There's a Monster in My Closet.*

    What do you think this poem is about?

    What clues did the poet give you about the mystery?

3. Discuss with your family: What is an item at home that we could turn into "a monster."

    Write a short story or poem about the monster you created.

    Check the list: *What Makes a Story Scary?* to help write about the mysterious object.

    Draw a picture of your "monster."

4. Be ready to share your story and picture with others.

Help! There's a Monster in My Closet

There's a monster in my closet.
He lives behind the door.
It's quiet and it's dark in there.
He doesn't even snore!

But my mama takes him out sometimes.
That's what really makes me shake!
She plugs his tail into the wall
And he roars like an earthquake.

He sucks down at the carpet
It's a frightful sight to see.
He goes at it so hungrily,
He might even suck up me!

That's when I run away and hide
But I still can hear him moan.
When a monster's running through your house
There's no place to be alone.

I'm shaking and I'm quaking
And I think that it's the end.
Then suddenly, a miracle!
All's quiet once again.

Now he's back inside the closet
And from beneath the bed I'll creep
And check behind the closet door
To make sure he's fast asleep.

I spy his name across his chest.
It's written there to see.
My monster's name is Hoover.
Please Hoover, don't eat me!

By Barbara Emaus

Retrieved 1/07 from www.ttlntl.co.uk/2/Poems/monster.htm.

Classroom and Home Connection

After *Scary Stories Family Night*, teachers may conduct a class lesson on writing a scary story so that all students, including those who could not attend, can build their writing skills in this genre.

- Discuss the list of authors' techniques: *What Makes a Story Scary?*
- Ask students who attended *Scary Stories Family Night* to share something they heard, wrote, or learned.
- Start with "story starters." Students may add a sentence to a story orally or in writing, individually or as a team.
- Stories may be completed for homework and read aloud at home for family partners to enjoy.

Students may choose from scary-story-starters, such as:

- It was a cold Halloween night.
- The mad scientist was creating a new monster.
- I got an eerie feeling when I heard…
- A mysterious object was floating in the air.
- Something in the closet was making a strange noise.
- The black cat started to crouch and hiss.
- OR, make up your own scary story starter.

Resource: Story starters adapted from *A Cauldron of Halloween Ideas,* by Lorrie Birchall at: http://teacher.scholastic.com/lessonrepro/lessonplans/profbooks/starters.htm

Explore the Community

At *Scary Stories Family Night,* talk with families about previewing scary movies they rent or see to make sure they are age-appropriate. Encourage families to talk with their children about what made a movie scary.

CHAPTER 4

Family Funny Reading Night
(November)

Family Funny Reading Night celebrates reading for enjoyment. Students, parents, and other members of the family can enjoy being silly together and finding the humor in jokes, riddles, songs, and funny stories.

The evening includes a whole group activity on riddles, student presentation of silly songs, and primary and intermediate grades creative writing about funny characters.

Riddle-Dee-Dee!
(Whole Group)

Students and families will read and solve riddles together. They also may enjoy joke books, riddle books, and other humorous books that are displayed in the room. They may create their own riddles to share with others.

Materials

- *Family Page: Riddle-Dee-Dee!*
  Teacher-leader will hold the answers to the riddles until the end of the activity.

  Answers to *Family Page* of riddles:

1. Because it follows the C	6. Because he lost his patients	11. An address
2. You are putting me on	7. Close the door, I'm dressing	12. Blubber gum
3. A yolk book	8. A screwdriver	13. Shall we go for a dip?
4. For holding up the pants	9. A yardstick	14. Hello, sucker
5. 24 cents	10. When the joker is wild	

- Collection of joke books, riddle books, and humorous books in the room.

Skills Reinforced

- Using context clues
- Developing vocabulary

SILLY SONGS (STUDENT PRESENTATION)

Prior to *Family Funny Reading Night*, select a class or grade level to perform a familiar, funny song. Some examples include: *Do Your Ears Hang Low?*, *On Top of Spaghetti*, and *John Jacob Jingleheimer Schmidt*. Or, select another silly or happy song to represent the theme for the night.

Alternatively, students may start with a well-known silly song and add original verses. For example, *On Top of Spaghetti* may be extended with new verses such as "Inside the Green Salad," "Deep in the Soup Bowl," and so on.

At *Family Funny Reading Night*, provide copies of the lyrics to all participants. Students will perform first, and then lead a sing-a-long.

See other humorous songs and lyrics at:
http://www.bussongs.com/silly_songs.php
http://www.head-start.lane.or.us/education/activities/music/songs-silly.html

Riddle-Dee-Dee!
(Whole Group)

Riddles are fun and funny! As a family, read the riddles below and solve as many as you can.

1. Why is the letter D like a sailor?

2. What did the sock say to the foot?

3. What do you call a funny book about eggs?

4. Why was the belt arrested?

5. What is the difference between a new penny and an old quarter?

6. Why did the doctor switch jobs?

7. What did the mayonnaise say to the mustard?

8. What driver doesn't have a license?

9. What has one foot on each side and one in the middle?

10. When is it dangerous to play cards?

11. What clothing does a house wear?

12. What do whales like to chew?

13. What did one potato chip say to the other?

14. What did the chocolate bar say to the lollipop?

When you finish, write another riddle and answer that you know or create a new one.

Riddle: _____

_____

Answer: _____

_____

You may read other joke and riddle books in the room.

If your family likes solving riddles, borrow riddle books from the school library or public library, or visit this Web site for riddles: http://www.justriddlesandmore.com/lettriddles.html

Amelia Bedelia Comes to Our Home (K-2)

Materials

- A book from the *Amelia Bedelia* series by Peggy Parish
- Writing paper
- Pencils
- Drawing paper
- Crayons and markers
- *Family Page: Amelia Bedelia Comes to Our Home*

Skills Reinforced

- Determining cause and effect
- Identifying main idea and detail

Activity

1. Read an Amelia Bedelia story aloud.

2. Ask the whole group: What makes this story funny? Explain that people think different things are funny. See if the students and families mention these common features of funny stories. List them on a board, chart, or include them on the *Family Page*.

   ### What Makes Something Funny?
   - Something unexpected happens
   - Something silly happens
   - Something is exaggerated
   - Something impossible happens

   Students and families may have other good ideas. They may mention funny language, surprises, tricks played on characters, clever things happen, or other things that make them laugh. Add their ideas to the list.

3. Ask participants to pretend that Amelia Bedelia came to visit and help them. Think of something funny that might happen at your home if she tried to help. Use the *Family Page: Amelia Bedelia Comes To Our Home* for students and families to write about and illustrate something funny that might happen.

4. Select a few students to share their stories and pictures with the group.

Amelia Bedelia Comes to Our Home (K-2)

We listened to one of the *Amelia Bedelia* books by author Peggy Parish. Did your family like it? What did you think was the funniest part?

Now, you and your family can add to the funny Amelia stories with your own example. Pretend that Amelia Bedelia came to help your family. Talk together about what funny things might happen in your home.

Think of three things you could ask her to do.

How might she follow your directions in a silly or unexpected way?

If we asked Amelia to...	She might...
Dust the furniture...	Sprinkle baby powder on the furniture to <u>PUT</u> dust on it!
1.	
2.	
3.	

Would you like having Amelia Bedelia in your home? Why or why not?

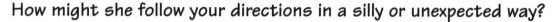

_____

_____

_____

Use your list of ideas to write a short story with a few good sentences about Amelia Bedelia's visit to your home.

Use the drawing paper and art supplies to illustrate one funny thing that happened.

We will share our funny stories and pictures.

Silly Super-Duper Heroes Have Some Fun! (3-5)

Materials

- One *Captain Underpants** book by Dav Pilkey
- Pencils
- Drawing paper

Skills Reinforced

- Determining main ideas and details
- Identifying character traits

Activity

1. Ask the students and families to name some of their favorite superheroes. Add *Captain Underpants*, if he is not named.

2. Read a funny section from one of the *Captain Underpants* books by Dav Pilkey.

3. Discuss with students and families: What makes a story funny? Explain that people think different things are funny. See if the students and families mention these common features of funny stories. List them on a board, chart, or include them on the *Family Page*.

    What Makes Something Funny?
    - Something unexpected happens
    - Something silly happens
    - Something is exaggerated
    - Something impossible happens

    Students and families may have other good ideas. They may mention funny language, surprises, tricks played on characters, clever things that happen, or other things that make them laugh. Add their ideas to the list.

4. Discuss: Did Captain Underpants do something funny in this story? What was funniest to you? What made that funny?

5. Guide students and families to use the *Family Page* to write a short, Silly Super-Duper Hero story for Captain Underpants. Or, they may write a silly story about a well-known superhero *or* one they create (e.g., Daring Dog, Super Baby, Wonder Teacher). They will illustrate one funny thing in their story.

6. Arrange a Silly Super-Duper Hero walk-around so that students and families can see each others' stories and pictures. Ask two to three students to share their stories and pictures with the whole group.

*For more information on the *Captain Underpants* series of books by Dav Pilkey, visit: http://www.scholastic.com/captainunderpants/.

Silly Super-Duper Heroes Have Some Fun (3-5)

Did your family like the silly story about *Captain Underpants*? What did you think was the funniest part?

Now, you and your family can create another funny situation for *Captain Underpants*. Or, you can write your silly story about a famous superhero (e.g., Superman, Batman, Spiderman) or one that you make up (e.g., Daring Dog, Super Baby, Wonder Teacher, or one you name).

Think of a funny situation that calls for super powers. Now, plan a story:

Who is YOUR Silly Super-Duper Hero?_____

Where does your story take place? _____

Fill in the chart below to tell what will happen and how the Silly Super-Duper Hero will act in a funny way.

List two to three things that happen that call for super powers.	What funny things will YOUR Silly Super-Duper Hero do?
1.	
2.	
3.	

Use your list of ideas to write a short story of a few paragraphs on your Silly Super-Duper Hero's adventure.

Use the drawing paper and art supplies to illustrate one funny thing that happened.

We will share our funny stories and pictures.

Classroom and Home Connection

To follow up *Family Funny Reading Night*, teachers may ask all students to do the following homework assignment in Language Arts.

All students and their families get into funny situations. Ask students to interview a parent, grandparent, or older sister or brother with one of these questions:

Can you think of one funny thing that I did when I was a baby or little child?

What is one funny thing you did when you were my age?

Ask a grandparent: what is one funny thing my parent did at my age?

Students should summarize the funny situation in a few good sentences (primary grades) or paragraphs (intermediate grades) and illustrate the story.

Explore the Community

Remind students and families to look for riddle, joke, or humorous books at the school library, public library, or book store.

Teachers may duplicate the book list on p. 47 for families at *Family Funny Reading Night*. Also, give the list to students who were unable to attend.

FUNNY BOOKS THAT WILL KEEP THEM LAUGHING

Here are a few books that students may look for in the school or public library.

PRIMARY GRADES	INTERMEDIATE GRADES
Allard, Harry. **MISS NELSON IS MISSING** The kids in Room 207 take advantage of their teacher's good nature until she disappears and they are faced with a vile substitute.	Blume, Judy. **TALES OF A FOURTH GRADE NOTHING** Peter finds his demanding two-year-old brother an ever-increasing problem.
Butterworth, Nick. **JASPER'S BEANSTALK** Jasper hopes to grow a beanstalk, but becomes discouraged when the bean he plants doesn't grow after a week.	Manes, Stephen. **BE A PERFECT PERSON IN JUST THREE DAYS** Milo, tired of problems with his sister, parents, and classmates, finds a book in the library that promises to make him perfect in just three days.
De Paola, Tomie. **STREGA NONA** When Strega Nona leaves him alone with her magic pasta pot, Big Anthony is determined to show the townspeople how it works.	Pilkey, Dav. **THE ADVENTURES OF CAPTAIN UNDERPANTS** George and Harold hypnotize their principal into thinking that he is the Superhero Captain Underpants
Henkes, Kevin. **JULIUS, THE BABY OF THE WORLD** Lilly is convinced that the arrival of her new baby brother is the worst thing that has happened in their house until cousin Garland comes to visit.	Rockwell, Thomas. **HOW TO EAT FRIED WORMS** Two boys set out to prove that worms can make a delicious meal.
Kimmel, Eric A. **I TOOK MY FROG TO THE LIBRARY** A young girl brings her pets to the library—with predictably disastrous results.	Sachar, Louis. **SIDEWAYS STORIES FROM WAYSIDE SCHOOL** Humorous episodes from the classroom on the thirtieth floor of Wayside School, which was accidentally built sideways with one classroom on each story.
Meddaugh, Susan. **MARTHA SPEAKS** Problems arise when Martha, the family dog, learns to speak after eating alphabet soup.	Scieszka, Jon. **THE TRUE STORY OF THE 3 LITTLE PIGS** The wolf gives his own outlandish version of what really happened when he tangled with the 3 little pigs.

These recommendations and more are provided by:

Monroe County Public Library, Indiana
   http://www.monroe.lib.in.us/childrens/booklists/children_booklists.html

High Point Public Library, North Carolina
   http://www.highpointpubliclibrary.com and click on KIDS Good Books.

CHAPTER 5

Celebrations and Traditions Family Reading Night
(December)

Celebrations and Traditions Family Reading Night helps students and families explore, discuss, and understand different holidays and customs. Although holidays occur throughout the year, December is a good time for this Family Reading Night.[1]

This event includes a whole group activity for children and families to talk about their own and others' celebrations throughout the year, a student presentation of songs and poems, and activities for the primary and intermediate grades that promote discussions of common and diverse traditions.

Many Reasons to Celebrate!
(Whole Group)

Students and families will work together on several fun activities that encourage discussions about many holidays and traditions. Participants can work as individual families or with others at their tables.

Materials

- *Family Pages:*
  Holiday Word Find
  Name that Holiday
  Match the Holiday and Custom
- Crayons and/or markers

Skills Reinforced

- Developing vocabulary
- Summarizing ideas

CELEBRATE GOOD TIMES (STUDENT PRESENTATION)

Prior to *Celebrations and Traditions Family Reading Night*, ask students from one class or grade level to prepare appropriate and diverse holiday songs that will be of interest to all major groups at the school. Ideas for songs may be found at:

www.bussongs.com/holiday_songs.php
Traditional holiday songs/elementary grades

www.nancymusic.com/Holiday.htm
Words and sheet music/original songs for all major December holidays

www.preschooleducation.com/sholiday.shtml
Original songs/kindergarten

At *Celebrations and Traditions Family Reading Night*, a Teacher-Leader may welcome everyone with the poem, *Celebrations*.[2]

Provide the lyrics of the songs the students sing to all participants. First, the audience will listen to the students sing. Then, the students may conduct a sing-a-long for everyone to sing one or more songs.

Holiday Word Find
(Whole Group)

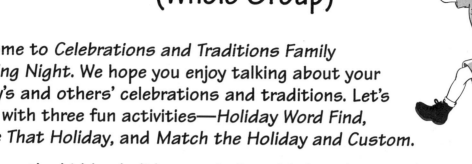

Welcome to *Celebrations and Traditions Family Reading Night.* We hope you enjoy talking about your family's and others' celebrations and traditions. Let's begin with three fun activities—*Holiday Word Find, Name That Holiday,* and *Match the Holiday and Custom.*

Discover the hidden holiday words listed below the puzzle. You can go up, down, forward, diagonally, or backwards!

```
O  F  F  R  Y  J  S  Z  B  G  O  G  U  H  E
T  B  E  P  L  E  F  A  M  I  L  Y  V  M  N
U  B  V  A  H  E  U  B  A  G  X  W  E  E  J
G  P  D  T  S  E  W  H  T  O  H  R  W  P  O
E  B  O  R  P  T  I  L  G  A  V  W  L  C  Y
N  L  D  Z  S  Q  R  R  S  X  A  P  E  X  Y
C  X  N  O  D  O  O  F  G  N  D  S  S  O  A
Z  R  N  O  U  A  Z  Q  Z  F  C  M  E  V  D
C  G  K  Z  I  Y  J  S  T  O  A  U  U  W  I
S  Z  F  P  J  T  T  H  R  V  X  R  F  M  L
I  K  K  X  H  C  I  U  O  D  J  W  B  Y  O
N  Y  I  O  N  M  J  D  X  G  D  Y  M  W  H
U  U  Z  O  D  S  P  O  A  Y  M  C  D  L  J
E  T  A  R  B  E  L  E  C  R  G  H  B  K  W
K  B  R  P  B  U  F  J  Q  X  T  H  K  J  P
```

CELEBRATE	CLOTHES	ENJOY
FAMILY	FEAST	FOOD
HOLIDAY	SONGS	TRADITION

Created with Puzzlemaker at www.DiscoverySchool.com—see Build Word Search.

Name That Holiday
(Whole Group)

How many holiday pictures can you identify? What other symbols, or activities come to mind for these holidays? Skip any you do not know.

_____

_____

_____

_____

_____

_____

_____

_____

_____

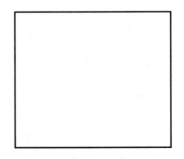

_____

_____

Draw a symbol for another holiday your family celebrates.

Match the Holiday and Custom
(Whole Group)

With your family, draw a line from each <u>holiday</u> to the <u>custom</u> that goes with it. Discuss: Do you celebrate each holiday in this way or some other way?

HOLIDAY	CUSTOM
Labor Day	Dye eggs
Halloween	Trim a tree
Thanksgiving	Celebrate the work that people do
Christmas	Honor past presidents
Hanukkah	Say, "trick or treat!"
Kwanzaa	Celebrate equality for all
Ramadan	Buy mom a gift
New Year's Day	Buy dad a gift
Chinese New Year	Fast during the day for a month
Martin Luther King Day	Eat potato latkes (pancakes)
Valentine's Day	Eat a turkey
President's Day	Watch fireworks
Easter	Honor soldiers in past wars
Memorial Day	Honor seven symbols
Mother's Day	Make a resolution to improve
Father's Day	Make a heart card
4th of July	Mark the Year of the Dragon

Discuss with your family and others at your table:
Which is your favorite holiday in the year? Why?

Draw a picture that shows how your family celebrates one of your favorite holidays. See if others can guess the holiday in your picture.

A Favorite Celebration (K-2)

Materials

- Book that highlights a family holiday celebration along with excellent illustrations, such as:
  Bunny Christmas: A Family Celebration by Rick Walton
  Seven Candles for Kwanzaa by Andrea Davis Pinkney
- *Family Page: A Favorite Celebration*
- Pencils, crayons, and/or markers

Skills Reinforced

- Summarizing information
- Identifying main idea and detail

Activity

1. Read aloud a good, short picture book that showcases a family sharing a holiday tradition. Discuss the tradition in the book with the whole group.

   Ask: Does your family have a tradition that you enjoy? How is your tradition the same or different from the one in the story?

2. Guide students and families to use the *Family Page: A Favorite Celebration* and complete the activity.

3. Bring the group back together. Ask a few families to share their ideas with the whole group.

A Favorite Celebration (K-2)

Holidays change our day-to-day routines and add pleasure to our lives. What are your family's favorite holidays? Talk about your favorites, then fill in ideas for one holiday that you want to tell more about.

One of my family's favorite holidays is: _____

On this holiday, one thing we do to celebrate is: _____

Some activities are "traditions" that are repeated every year. What is one family tradition on this holiday? _____

Why do you like this holiday? _____

Draw a picture of how you and your family celebrate this holiday.

Write a sentence that tells something about the picture.

_____

_____

_____

My Family-Your Family: Favorite Holidays (3-5)

Materials

- *Family Page: My Family-Your Family: Favorite Holidays*
- Pencils, crayons and/or markers
- Drawing paper

Skills Reinforced

- Taking notes
- Comparing and contrasting information

Activity

1. Guide students and families to use the *Family Page: My Family-Your Family: Favorite Holidays*. Start with Part 1: Family Discussion. Students will talk with their own family about holidays they enjoy and take notes about one favorite holiday. They may draw a picture of how they celebrate the selected holiday on the back of the page or on drawing paper.

2. After about 20 minutes, direct the students and families to move to Part 2, an interview with another family at their table or nearby who selected a **different** holiday as their favorite. The student will ask the other family a few questions, take notes, and compare holiday traditions.

   If time permits, guide students to interview a second family and take notes on the back of the page.

3. In the final 20 minutes, lead a whole-group discussion with students and families on similarities and differences that they noted as they compared their family's traditions and celebrations with others. Ask questions such as.

   - What did you hear that is the SAME as something your family does?
   - What did you hear that is DIFFERENT from what your family does?
   - Why is it important to learn about many celebrations?

4. See the Web sites in Chapter Notes for summaries and short stories on holidays throughout the year.[3]

My Family-Your Family: Favorite Holidays (3-5)

Part 1. Family Discussion

Holidays add interest and pleasure to our lives. With your family, discuss: What are our favorite holidays?

Fill in ideas about <u>one</u> holiday that your family enjoys.

One of my family's favorite holidays is: _____

On this holiday, one thing we do to celebrate is: _____

_____

This is our favorite holiday because: _____

_____

On a separate paper, draw a picture of how you and your family celebrate this holiday.

. . . .

Part 2. Interview

Meet with a family nearby who wrote about a *different holiday.*
Take notes on these questions:

What holiday did you hear about? _____

Why does the family like this holiday? _____

What is one way that they celebrate? _____

Does YOUR family celebrate THIS holiday? If so, how is your family's celebration the same or different from the family you interviewed?

_____

_____

Be ready to share.

Classroom and Home Connection

Holidays are times when families enjoy traditional foods. Before or after *Celebrations and Traditions Family Reading Night*, ask students to talk with a parent about a favorite recipe that they could share in a *Holiday Cook Book*.

- As a homework assignment, have students write the recipe and illustrate what the food looks like.

- Compile the recipes in a class or grade-level booklet, including holiday treats from all cultures in the school.

- If this is a winter project, the book might include Christmas cookies, latkes for Hanukkah, etc.

- If holidays are explored at other times of the year, the recipes may include other specialties (e.g., edible eyeballs for Halloween, Easter cupcakes, Ramadan specialties, etc.).

- Make copies of the book for all students and their families.

Explore the Community

Ask students to interview someone in the community to learn about other people's favorite holidays throughout the year and their most memorable traditions. The person may be someone with a different cultural background or a senior citizen who grew up in a different era. If this is difficult in your school's neighborhood, invite a panel of diverse adults to the class for students to interview as a whole class.

Chapter Notes

1. The planning committee for Family Reading Nights should discuss whether the theme of winter celebrations and traditions will be enjoyed and appreciated in the school or create difficulties. In some schools, it will help to set the stage for reading and discussing winter holidays.

2. Before students present songs that honor diverse holidays, teacher-leaders may welcome families with the following poem or with comments about the richness of diverse cultures in the school.

Celebrations

It is December—a good time for a celebration.
Many traditions are honored across the nation.
At this *Family Reading Night* we will learn
How all families celebrate, and we will earn
A better understanding of our diverse school.
The evening provides us with a useful tool
To respect and honor the cultures of others
So we treat our classmates like sisters and brothers.

Let the celebration begin! We will explore
Cultures, traditions, holidays, and more.
If we miss your tradition, please plan to share—
We must understand all cultures. We really *do* care!
Holidays through the year will help us know
Many ways to celebrate—so, ready, set, let's go!

—Marsha D. Greenfeld, 2006

3. Summary stories of various winter (and other) holidays are found on the following Web sites.

   http://www.educationworld.com/holidays/archives/december.shtml
   Education World offers resources to help educators teach about the special days in December.

   http://www.holidays.net/
   Holidays on the Net provides multimedia information on many holidays, including their histories and holiday-related activities.

   http://www.infoplease.com/spot/winterholidays1.html
   This Web site offers information about all the major seasonal holidays.

CHAPTER 6

Reading Olympics Family Night
(January)

Children need not wait four years for the Olympics. They can participate in a Reading Olympics every year. *Reading Olympics Family Night* reinforces students' reading and language arts skills with activities and games that are fun for students, families, and educators.

This evening event includes a whole group activity and student performance for an Opening Ceremony, a series of reading and literacy game stations, and Reading Olympics medals at a Closing Ceremony.

Family Flags (Whole Group)

Families use art supplies and a Family Page to create a family flag about their favorite reading and writing activities to display in the Opening Ceremonies of the *Reading Olympics Family Night*.

Materials

- Crayons or markers
- 11 x 17 drawing paper
  The paper may be cut in the shape of a pennant and pre-lined for three sections for students' drawings.

Skills Reinforced

- Following directions
- Speaking clearly

LET THE GAMES BEGIN! (STUDENT PRESENTATION)

Prior to *Reading Olympics Family Night*, select one class or grade level to practice a song, play music, or perform a dance suitable for the Olympic Games. The performance should be short—no more than 10 minutes. See Chapter Notes on p. 72 for ideas.

Opening Ceremonies

1. The principal, chair of the planning committee, or other official will welcome everyone to *Reading Olympics Family Night*. The leader may ask students and families about their favorite sports in the Olympics, and describe *Reading Olympics Family Night* as a time to enjoy reading games.

2. Students will perform for the Opening Ceremonies after dinner and after most families complete their Family Flags in the Whole Group Activity.

3. After the entertainment, families will walk around the room and display their Family Flags in an Olympic entry march. Consider playing marching music in the background as families carry their flags.

4. Family Flags may be hung in the room and, later, some may be displayed in the school lobby or on a bulletin board.

Family Flags (Whole Group)

Welcome to *Reading Olympics Family Night!*
You have come to these Olympic games to enjoy
reading and writing together. By the end of the
evening, you will have a Reading Olympics Medal
for your good work. Before we begin, you need a
Family Flag for the Opening Ceremonies.

1. Discuss your family member's favorite reading
   activities. These could include favorite books,
   magazines, writing, word games, newspapers,
   comics or other ways that you enjoy reading and writing at home.

   What are your family's favorite reading activities?

   _____   _____

   _____   _____

   _____   _____

2. As a family, decide how each person's favorite reading activities
   will be displayed on your flag. Choose 3 IDEAS to show in the
   three sections of your flag.

3. Use the art materials provided to create a Reading Olympics
   Family Flag. Students should draw at least one section of the
   flag. Other family members may also draw sections of the flag.
   Remember: Keep your flag simple! Just 3 favorite reading activities.

4. Talk with others at your table and share what your family put on the
   flag. You will march with your Family Flag in the Reading Olympics
   Opening Ceremonies.

How to Arrange Reading Olympics

Reading Olympics Family Night is arranged as a series of stations that are facilitated by a teacher or adult volunteer. All activities must be appropriate for students in the primary *and* intermediate grades. Each game will take about 10 minutes. Then, each group of students and families will move to the next station.

Activity Stations

Arrange four Reading Olympic games around a large room or, to minimize noise, put one activity in four classrooms that are near each other. Have a teacher or volunteer facilitate each station.

At Reading Olympics Family Night

1. Facilitator will explain to the participants how *Reading Olympics Family Night* will work before assigning students and families to four groups. Give each family an Olympic Events Card to identify their group (e.g., yellow, green, red, and blue). The groups will move together from game to game.

2. Families will rotate through four stations, moving to a new game every 10 minutes. Label the stations 1, 2, 3, 4 so that families will move from one to the next in order. The signs for each game (on yellow, green, red, and blue paper) will guide each group to their first location. Then, they will follow directions to cycle through the game stations.

3. At the end of each game, leaders will mark each family's Olympic Events Card to show how many activities the families completed.

4. At the Closing Ceremonies (or before they leave), families will exchange their Olympic Events Cards for a Reading Olympics Family Night Medal. Templates for the Olympic Events Card and the Reading Olympics Family Night Medal are on p. 69 and p. 70.

Families Completing:	Receive this Medal:
4 Activities	Gold Medal
3 Activities	Silver Medal
2 Activities	Bronze Medal
1 Activity	Participation Medal

A to Z Race

Objective

Students and families will write categories of words in alphabetical order. Two to four games can be played in the 10-minute time period.

Materials

- White board and dry erase marker (one per family)
  Pencils and paper or index cards may be used if there are no white boards.
- Paper towel for dry eraser

Skills Reinforced

- Sequencing
- Spelling

Directions

1. Each family will use a white board, dry erase marker, and a paper towel eraser.

2. The Facilitator will call out a category, such as:
   - Animals
   - Foods/Fruits and Vegetables
   - Colors
   - U.S. States or Cities
   - Countries Around the World
   - Kinds of Cars or Transportation
   - Television Shows

3. Tell students and families:
   - I will give you a category to think about. When I say "Begin," work as a family to write as many words as you can that fit the category.

   - The words **must be written in alphabetical order**. So, think of an A word, B word, C word, and so on. OR, you may write your ideas leaving space for other ideas to fit in alphabetical order. You do not have to have a word for every letter of the alphabet. For example, if the category were colors, you might say A-Aqua, B-Blue, skip C, go to Dark Red, and so on.

   - You will have two minutes to write words for each category before we go on to a new one.

4. Give students and families the first category.

5. Call "Stop" after two minutes. Share information quickly about the number of words and the best or funniest answers.
   - Direct them to "Erase" and get ready for the next category.
   - Give students and families the next category.
   - After two minutes, again share ideas, erase, and go on to the next category.

6. Before the group moves to the next game, mark all Olympic Events Cards to record the families' participation in the A to Z Race.

Riddle Run

Objective

Families will work together to solve riddles.

Materials

- Pencils
- Page of riddles

  Planning Committee should prepare a page of about 20 riddles, from easy to difficult, without the answers. Teacher-Leaders will have an answer page. Find riddles in a book from the school library or see http://www.justriddlesandmore.com/lettriddles.html.

  See p. 41 for a page of riddles that can be used if that event is not planned.

Skills Reinforced

- Building vocabulary
- Improving comprehension

Directions

1. Give each family a page of riddles and a pencil.
2. Tell families:
   - When I say "Begin," work as a family to solve the riddles. The riddles are easy at first and then get more difficult. Write your answers to each riddle. Let's see how many riddles you can solve.
   - If you complete all of the riddles, your family may tell each other favorite riddles that you know. Or, write a riddle of your own on the back of your riddle page.
3. After 8 minutes call "Time." For the final two minutes, ask families to read their favorite riddles and answers from the page with the full group. There may be more than one good answer to the riddles.
4. Before the group moves to the next game, mark all Olympic Events Cards to record the families' participation in the Riddle Run.

Amazing Anagram Dash

Objective

Families will work together to find words in the phrase
READING OLYMPICS.

Materials

- Lined paper with **READING OLYMPICS** printed at the top in capital letters.
- Pencils

Skills Reinforced

- Spelling
- Building vocabulary

Directions

1. Each family will use a pencil and paper with the phrase
   R-E-A-D-I-N-G O-L-Y-M-P-I-C-S printed at the top.

2. Tell students and families:

   - When I say "Begin," work as a family to write words using only the letters in the phrase Reading Olympics.

   - Each word must be spelled correctly. You will have eight minutes for this game.

3. After five minutes call "Time." For the final five minutes, ask students and families to share two-letter, three-letter, four-letter words, the longest words, the best words, and the funniest words that they found. Find out how many found up to 10 words, 20 words, or more. Give a cheer for all participants!

4. Before the group moves to the next game, mark all Olympic Events Cards to record the families' participation in the Amazing Anagram Dash.

Word Chain Relay

Objective

Families will work together to generate a list of words by changing or adding only one letter at a time.

Materials

- Baskets for each table with 15 to 20 three-letter words written on individual large, lined index cards or folded, lined paper. Include words from different "word families," such as **cat, pet, tin, hop, run,** and so on. Place the same word cards in all of the baskets.
- Pencils

Skills Reinforced

- Spelling
- Applying phonics

Directions

1. Tell students and families:
   - When I say "Begin," each family will pick one card from the basket. Starting with the word on the card, the first family member will write a new word by changing or adding only ONE letter. For example, you could change ca**t** to ca**p**.
   - Take turns. The next family member will look at the new word and change or add only one letter to make another new word. In our example, the next person could change ca**p** to cap**e** or to c**u**p.
   - Continue taking turns to change any letter in the word chain until you have no more ideas. Then, pick a new card from the basket and start a new word chain. Take turns again to change or add one letter at a time to make new words. See how long you can make your word chains.
2. After eight minutes call "Time." For the final two minutes, ask students and families to read their word chains to show how they changed their words. Ask for a four-word chain, a five-word chain, the longest word chain, their favorite word chain, and so on.
3. Before the group moves to the next game, mark all Olympic Events Cards to record the families' participation in the Word Chain Relay.

Olympic Events Cards

Use these Olympic Events Cards (or an equivalent design) to show the events that families complete. Facilitators will check (✓) the circle next to each event, as the families leave the room to go to the next game.

Copy the cards on cardstock for durability. Use colors to show the groups of families who will travel together from game to game.

OLYMPIC EVENTS CARD

○ **A to Z Race**
○ **Riddle Run**
○ **Amazing Anagram Dash**
○ **Word Chain Relay**

OLYMPIC EVENTS CARD

○ **A to Z Race**
○ **Riddle Run**
○ **Amazing Anagram Dash**
○ **Word Chain Relay**

OLYMPIC EVENTS CARD

○ **A to Z Race**
○ **Riddle Run**
○ **Amazing Anagram Dash**
○ **Word Chain Relay**

OLYMPIC EVENTS CARD

○ **A to Z Race**
○ **Riddle Run**
○ **Amazing Anagram Dash**
○ **Word Chain Relay**

Reading Olympics Family Night Medals

Use these templates (or the equivalent) for the Reading Olympics Medals that families receive at the Closing Ceremonies. Write the name of the school on the line. Then, copy on appropriately colored paper for gold, silver, bronze, and participation medals. Use heavy cardstock or laminate the medals for durability.

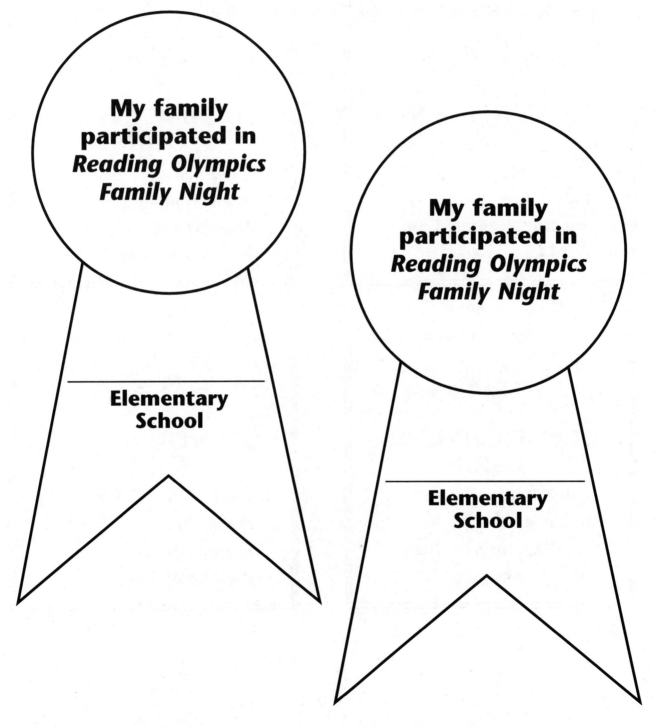

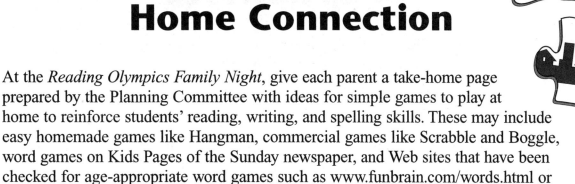

Classroom and Home Connection

At the *Reading Olympics Family Night*, give each parent a take-home page prepared by the Planning Committee with ideas for simple games to play at home to reinforce students' reading, writing, and spelling skills. These may include easy homemade games like Hangman, commercial games like Scrabble and Boggle, word games on Kids Pages of the Sunday newspaper, and Web sites that have been checked for age-appropriate word games such as www.funbrain.com/words.html or www.aolatschool.com/students.

Do not include games that are expensive or difficult to find or develop. Separate lists may be made for students in the primary and intermediate grades.

Explore the Community

Invite a local amateur or professional athlete to speak at *Reading Olympics Family Night*. Ask him or her to share information on setting goals, training, and how reading connects to success. Arrange for the speaker well in advance to ensure a commitment and to allow time for a backup speaker, if that is necessary.

Chapter Notes

STUDENT PRESENTATION. The student presentation should be planned at least two weeks before the Reading Olympics Family Night. A class or grade level may prepare to:

    a) Sing a motivating song, such as *Climb Every Mountain*.

    b) Change the words to a well-known sports song, such as turning *Take Me Out the Ball Game* into ***Take Me Out to the Olympic Games***

    c) Play a march with classroom instruments, kazoos, or band instruments.

NUMBER OF GAME STATIONS. The four stations described in this chapter will serve up to 40 people. For example, 10 students and family members may go to each station, and then move from station to station every 10 minutes. If more than 40 people are registered for *Reading Olympics Family Night*, the planning committee should add more game stations for each group of 10. Or, duplicate game stations may be used with primary and intermediate grades students and families. Teacher-Leaders may add favorite literacy games or see www.educationworld.com for reading and language arts activities that may be designed as Olympic game stations. If more or different game stations are added, the Olympic Events Cards and directions to families must be revised.

LOCATION. Reading Olympic game stations may be arranged around a large cafeteria or gymnasium, or, to control noise, may be located in four classrooms in close proximity to ensure easy transitions from game to game.

SUPERVISION. At least one teacher or adult leader is needed for each game station. One Teacher-Leader should facilitate the opening and closing ceremonies. Another Teacher-Leader should remain in a central location to distribute the Reading Olympics Medals to families who leave early or at the closing ceremony. If many adult volunteers are available, they may "co-lead" activities as the groups rotate from station to station.

WHOLE GROUP ACTIVITY: FAMILY FLAGS. One or two sample flags may be shown to give students and families a few ideas of how to draw their favorite reading activities in large and colorful ways.

ABC RACE. Dry erase boards may be made from "shower board." Shower board may be purchased and cut to size at a low cost at Home Depot.

RIDDLE RUN. School and public libraries have books of riddles for the planning committee to create a page of about 20 riddles to be distributed to all families. Or, see these Web sites for riddles and answers: www.justriddlesandmore.com and www.brownielocks.com/riddles.html.

CLOSING CEREMONIES. Some families will leave early. They should stop by a central location to pick up their Reading Olympics Medals. If there is time, bring everyone together for an official Closing Ceremonies:

    ■ Thank everyone for coming, lead a final cheer, sing a school song, and present the participation medals to each student for the family.

    ■ Ask students and families which activities they liked best; something they learned from the different games; which game they could play at home; and other reflective questions.

    ■ Have students and families complete an evaluation of the event with their suggestions for improvements.

LINK FAMILY INVOLVEMENT TO SCHOOL READING CHALLENGES. Many schools conduct programs to encourage students to meet reading targets during a school year, such as reading 10,000 books for pleasure or reading one million words or pages. A *Reading Olympics Family Night* could link family and community involvement to the reading challenge.

CHAPTER 7

Stories and Tales Family Night
(February)

Students and families like to read and listen to folk tales and fairy tales. Old stories can help students think about things in new ways, teach a lesson, demonstrate an important value, or simply entertain.

This event includes a whole group activity that reminds families of the tales they know, a student creative drama presentation, and activities for the primary and secondary grades that reinforce reading and writing.

Famous Story Clues
(Whole Group)

Families will read a list of clues about well-known fairy tales, talk together about the stories, and find the clue that has nothing to do with the story. They also may draw a picture of one of their favorite tales.

Materials

- Paper table tents naming one fairy tale should identify each table, such as:

Hansel and Gretel	The Emperor's New Clothes
Cinderella	Snow White and the Seven Dwarfs
Little Red Riding Hood	Sleeping Beauty
Little Red Hen	The Gingerbread Boy
Three Little Pigs	Other favorites
Jack and the Beanstalk	

- *Family Page: Famous Story Clues*
- Crayons and/or markers
- Drawing paper

Skills Reinforced

- Identifying main ideas and details

NEW KIDS TELL AN OLD TALE (STUDENT PRESENTATION)

Prior to *Stories and Tales Family Night*, select one class to give a creative dramatic presentation of a short fairy tale, such as *Three Billy Goats Gruff* (see http://www.funpagesforkids.com/billy/), *Goldilocks and the Three Bears* (see http://www.dltk-kids.com/rhymes/goldilocks_story.htm), or a folk tale or fairy tale chosen by the class.

Creative dramatics do not require fancy costumes or formal scripts. Students interpret a story with just a few key props. Usually, only one rehearsal is needed prior to the presentation at *Stories and Tales Family Night*. The presentation should take no more than 15 minutes.

Famous Story Clues
(Whole Group)

Welcome to *Stories and Tales Family Reading Night.*
We hope you enjoy the strange, wonderful world of
fairy tales.

1. Look at the clues for each fairy tale below.
   Talk over the stories with your family.
   One clue *does* NOT belong. Circle the clue that
   has nothing to do with the story.

   <u>Hansel and Gretel</u>: bread crumbs, stepmother,
   hen, oven, chicken bone

   <u>Cinderella</u>: mice, beach, ball gown, shoes,
   stepsisters, prince

   <u>Little Red Riding Hood</u>: basket, woods, wolf,
   new shoes, grandmother

   <u>The Three Little Pigs</u>: eggs, house, huffing, wolf, straw, brick

   <u>Goldilocks and the Three Bears</u>: porridge, wolf, woods, bed,
   chair, baby

   <u>Little Red Hen</u>: help, bread, flour, lazy, winter, wheat

   <u>Jack and the Beanstalk</u>: cow, fee-fi-fo-fum, giant, harp,
   magic, silk

   <u>Sleeping Beauty</u>: apple, kiss, 100 years, forest, television,
   castle

   <u>Three Billy Goats Gruff</u>: bridge, troll, grass, biggest,
   teapot, clip-clop

   <u>The Gingerbread Boy</u>: sly, runs away, bakes, fast, fox, purple

2. Draw a picture that illustrates <u>ONE</u> of the fairy tales listed above.
   Try to include at least two of the story clues in your picture.

3. Show your picture to others at your table. Take turns telling the
   tales in your drawings.

My Side of the Story! (K-2)

Materials

- Short fairy tale for Teacher-Leader to read aloud
- *Family Page: Fairy Tale Characteristics*
- *Family Page: Write a Friendly Letter*

Skills Reinforced

- Writing a friendly letter
- Understanding a character's point of view

Activity

1. Ask the group about their favorite fairy tales. Talk over the Resource Page of *Fairy Tale Characteristics* with the students and families. This page may be distributed or posted as a chart for all to see.

2. Tell the students and families that you will read one tale, and that they should listen to hear the *Fairy Tale Characteristics* in the story.

   Read a short, familiar fairy tale to the group, such as *Goldilocks and the Three Bears*, *The Little Red Hen*, *Little Red Riding Hood*, or a similar story.

3. Choose one character from the story. With students and families, discuss the events of the story and what they think about the character's actions. What was the character thinking? Did the character use good judgment? For example, depending on the story read, discuss the following questions...

   a. With *Goldilocks*: Do you think Goldilocks should have eaten the bear's porridge? Why or why not?

   b. With the *Little Red Hen*: Why did the hen get angry at her friends? Do you think she was right not to share her bread? What would you have done?

   c. With *Little Red Riding Hood*: Why didn't Little Red Riding Hood listen to her mother? What advice would you give her?

   ...Or similar questions based on the story that is read aloud.

4. Ask the students and families to think of one of their favorite fairy or folk tales and to select a character in the story. They will write a friendly letter to that character about their actions in the story. They may give advice, ask questions, or offer comments. Use the *Family Page: Write a Friendly Letter*.

5. Ask all students and families to check the key parts of their letters: Did they put a comma after the greeting and closing? Did they have a capital letter at the start of each new sentence? and so on. Invite a few students to read their letters to the whole group.

Write a Friendly Letter (K-2)

We listened to a famous fairy tale and talked about the behavior of one character. Now, as a family, write a friendly letter to a character in one of YOUR favorite fairy tales.

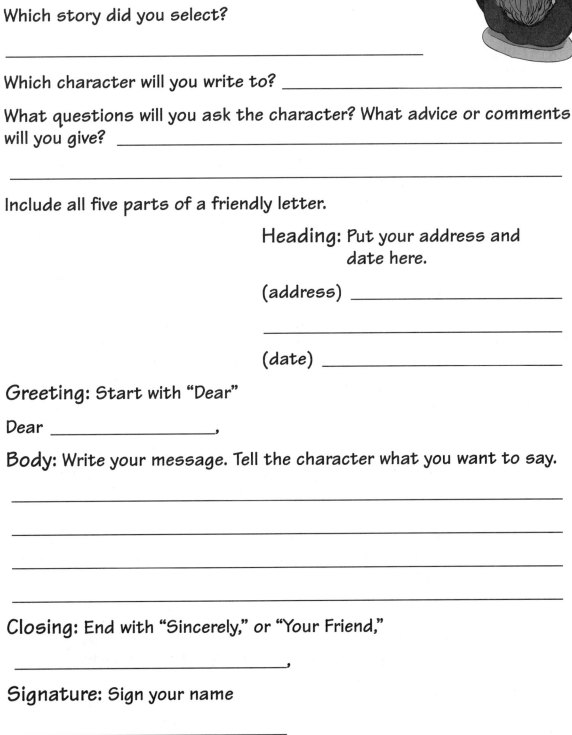

Which story did you select?

_____

Which character will you write to? _____

What questions will you ask the character? What advice or comments will you give? _____

_____

Include all five parts of a friendly letter.

Heading: Put your address and date here.

(address) _____

_____

(date) _____

Greeting: Start with "Dear"

Dear _____,

Body: Write your message. Tell the character what you want to say.

_____

_____

_____

_____

Closing: End with "Sincerely," or "Your Friend,"

_____,

Signature: Sign your name

_____

Believe It or Not! (3-5)

Materials

- Book for Teacher-Leader to read
- *Family Page: Fairy Tale Characteristics* (see p. 81)
- *Family Page: Write a Friendly Letter*

Skills Reinforced

- Writing a friendly letter
- Understanding a character's point of view

Activity

1. Ask the group about their favorite fairy tales. Talk over the *Family Page: Fairy Tale Characteristics* with the students and families. This page may be distributed or posted as a chart for all to see.

2. Tell the students and families that you will read a different kid of tale—a "twisted tale." They should listen for the *Fairy Tale Characteristics* in the story.

   Read a twisted fairy tale aloud, such as *The True Story of the 3 Little Pigs* by John Sciezka, or *The Three Little Wolves and the Big Bad Pig* by Eugene Triviza.

3. Discuss with the students and families what makes the story a fairy tale.

   In twisted tales, the author changes the point of view of the story. For example, usually readers sympathize with the three little pigs. In the twisted tale, readers hear the wolf's side of the story. Discuss the events of the revised story.

4. Ask students and families to talk with each other about whether or not they are convinced by the wolf's version of the story. Does he seem trustworthy? Why or why not?

5. Guide students and families to write a friendly letter to Mr. Wolf about whether they agree with his point of view and claims of innocence.* They may give advice, ask questions, or offer comments. Use the *Family Page: Write a Friendly Letter*.

6. Ask students and families to check the key parts of their letters: Did they put a comma after the greeting and closing? Did they have a capital letter at the start of each new sentence? and so on. Invite a few students to share their letters with the whole group.

*Adapted from: http://teacher.scholastic.com/writewit/mff/fractured_fairy_true.htm.
 See information on the author, Jon Sciezka and *The True Story of the Three Little Pigs*.

Write a Friendly Letter (3-5)

In the "twisted" tale, we heard Mr. Wolf's version of the story of the three little pigs. Did you believe it? Do you think Mr. Wolf was as good as he said? With your family, write a letter to Mr. Wolf. You may ask him questions, give advice, or let him know if you think he will win his case and why. First, plan what you will write.

What questions will you ask Mr. Wolf?

_____

What advice, comments, or messages will you give Mr. Wolf?

_____

Remember to include all five parts of a friendly letter.

Heading: Put your address and date here.

_____

_____

_____

Greeting: Start with "Dear"

Dear _____ ,

Body: Write your message. Tell the character what you want to say.

_____

_____

_____

Closing: End with "Sincerely," or "Your Friend,"

_____ ,

Signature: Sign your name

_____

Classroom and Home Connection

Teachers may build on *Stories and Tales Family Night* in class with all students, whether they attended the event with their families or not. Ask one student who was present to summarize a story that was read or a letter that was written.

Discuss with all students the list of *Fairy Tale Characteristics*. Although classic tales take place "a long time ago," students can use the same features to write a modern fairy tale. They may use kings, queens, giants, talking animals, and other fantastic creatures in a new fairy tale. People may become animals; things may come to life; and other magical events may occur to solve a problem.

Ask students to choose one of the following topics for their original tale or add other prompts.

1. A new kid comes to school
2. A new baby joins a family
3. A student finds money
4. A bully acts tough

5. Your best friend is moving away
6. You want to explore a new place
7. Grandmother is coming to visit
8. A situation you make up

Remind students to give the modern tale a good title and illustrate the story. The assignment may be written in class or completed for homework. Students should read their drafts aloud to a family partner for suggestions and reactions.

Explore the Community

Collaborate with the school or public library for students to read or tell their modern fairy tales to younger children.

Collaborate with a local senior citizens group to enable students to present creative dramatic versions of well-known fairy tales to a group of seniors.

Fairy Tale Characteristics* (K-5)

Listen to the fairy tale read by the Teacher-Leader.

Does the story have all or most of the following characteristics that are common in many fairy tales? Which of these did you hear about in the story?

- A special beginning such as: Once upon a time...

- A good character

- A bad or evil character

- Royalty (a king, queen, prince, princess) and/or a castle

- Magical people, animals, objects, or events

- Good magic or wicked magic

- A problem and a solution

- Things that happen in "threes" or "sevens"

- A special ending, such as: ...and they lived happily ever after.

*Adapted from: http://www.geocities.com/ljacoby_2000/fairytalechart.html, November 22, 2006.

CHAPTER 8

Dr. Seuss Family Night
(March)

Dr. Seuss's birthday is celebrated in many schools. Now, families can join the festivities. Participants will stretch their imaginations as they enter the remarkable world that Dr. Seuss created.

This event includes a whole-group activity to create an unusual zoo, a student performance as a readers' theater, and activities for families and students in the primary and intermediate grades based on Dr. Seuss's books.

Zany Zoo Animals
(Whole Group)

Family members will create an original, wacky animal inspired by characters from the book *If I Ran the Zoo* by Dr. Seuss.

The Teacher-Leader may enlarge one or two animals from *If I Ran the Zoo* for students and families to see as inspirations for creating their own animals.

The Teacher-Leader will exhibit the families' animals around the room in a **Zoo on the Wall**, and then read aloud *If I Ran the Zoo*.

Materials

- *If I Ran the Zoo*, by Dr. Seuss (copy for the Teacher-Leader)
- *Family Page: Zany Zoo Animals* (Directions)
- Crayons and/or markers
- Drawing paper or tagboard, 11 x 17 or larger. Teacher-Leaders may pre-line paper for title at the top and two sentences at the bottom.

Skills Reinforced

- Comparing and contrasting
- Creative thinking

DR. SEUSS FAVORITES (STUDENT PRESENTATION)
Activity

Prior to *Dr. Seuss Family Night*, select one intermediate grade or class to survey other students about their favorite Dr. Seuss books. Display the data on a bar graph, pictograph, or pie chart.

At *Dr. Seuss Family Night*, students will share how they collected the data, show the graph, and discuss the results.

The Teacher-Leader can poll the audience about their favorite Dr. Seuss books to see if the results match the graph of students' favorites.

Zany Zoo Animals
(Whole Group)

Welcome to *Dr. Seuss Family Night*. Tonight we are celebrating Dr. Seuss's birthday. To begin, let's do an activity that Dr. Seuss would have enjoyed.

1. Look around the room at the animals on display. They are zoo animals from *If I Ran the Zoo*.

2. Discuss with your family: If you ran a zoo, what wacky animals would be there?

3. Use the art supplies at your table to create an original animal that would be in your zoo. You may combine two, three, or more animals into a new one. Or, create an animal that was never seen before.

4. Give the animal you created a name that fits how it looks. Write its name on the line at the top of the page.

5. Underneath the picture, write two facts about your animal.

   You may imagine:

   ▪ What does your animal like to eat?

   ▪ Is your animal fast or slow?

   ▪ Which animals are its friends or enemies?

   ▪ Where does it live?

   ▪ Or other make-believe facts.

6. Display your animal in the Zoo on the Wall.

7. Walk around the room to see other animals in the zoo. How are they different from your animal? How are they the same?

   ▪ Which animal did you like best? _____

   _____

   ▪ Which animal was the funniest? _____

   _____

What Would You Do? (K-2)

Materials

- *The Cat in the Hat* by Dr. Seuss for the Teacher-Leader to read aloud.
- 11 x 17 drawing paper (story paper), with space for a picture and lines at the bottom of the page for writing a sentence.
- Crayons and/or markers
- Pencils
- *Family Page: What if the Cat in the Hat Visited You?*

Skills Reinforced

- Writing
- Listening

Activity

1. Ask the students what they like to do on rainy days at home.

2. Read *The Cat in the Hat* aloud to the participants.

3. Invite the students and families to share their reactions to *The Cat in the Hat*.

4. Use the *Family Page: What if the Cat in the Hat Visited You?*

   Ask the students: What would *you* do if the Cat in the Hat appeared at your door? Students will answer by drawing a picture and by writing a sentence to explain the picture.

5. When students finish their pictures and sentences, they will ask their family members for reactions. Ask the students and families to discuss: What would a parent do if the Cat in the Hat visited the home and left a mess?

6. Bring the group back together. Ask two to three students to show their pictures and read their sentences. Ask the students and parents to share their ideas about a visit from the Cat in the Hat.

What If the Cat in the Hat Visited You? (K-2)

In this activity, pretend that you are a character in *The Cat in the Hat*. What would you do if, one day, the Cat in the Hat appeared at your door?

1. Draw a large, colorful picture showing something you would do if the Cat in the Hat came to your home.

   Think about the following questions:

   ■ Would you play inside or outside?

   ■ Would you make a mess in a room or keep it clean?

   ■ Who would play with you?

2. At the bottom of the page, write one or two sentences to tell what is happening in your picture.

3. Discuss the following question with your family.

   What would your Mom or Dad do if they came home and found you playing with the Cat in the Hat?

4. Share your sentences, pictures, and ideas with others at your table and with the whole group.

What Would You See On Mulberry Street? (3-5)

Materials

- *And To Think That I Saw It On Mulberry Street* by Dr. Seuss for the Teacher-Leader to read aloud
- A Game Bag (e.g., bag, basket, envelope, or other container) (one per family)
- Game Words cut in strips and placed in the container for each family
- Lined paper
- Crayons and/or markers
- Mulberry Street Game Board
- *Family Page: What Would You See on Mulberry Street?*

Skills Reinforced

- Listening
- Writing

Activity

1. Before *Dr. Seuss Family Night*, make copies of the Mulberry Street Game Board for each family who will attend and prepare the Game Bags (containers) with Game Words for each family. Make a few extra boards and bags in case some families attend who did not register for the evening.

2. Read aloud *And To Think That I Saw It On Mulberry Street* to the students and families. Stop periodically to ask students questions such as:

   - How do you get to school (walk, bus, parent drives)?
   - What do you see on the way to school?
   - What would make your trip to school more interesting and exciting?

3. Students and their families will use *Family Page: What Would You See on Mulberry Street?* to play the Mulberry Street Game and create a list of outrageous animals, people, or things that might appear on their Game Board.

   Let students and families know that Dr. Seuss was all about imagination. Explain that each family will play a game that takes them on an imaginary walk on Mulberry Street. They will imagine what they *might* see along the way, and write short descriptions of the strange sights on their Game Boards.

4. Then, they will choose *one* of their imaginary sights to illustrate.

5. Gather the group together to share their descriptions and pictures of what they imagined on Mulberry Street.

What Would You See On Mulberry Street? (3-5)

Marco saw some pretty strange things on Mulberry Street! Each new sight was weirder than the one before.

Let's pretend that you and your family were walking along this unusual street. Imagine what you might add to Marco's list of wild and crazy sights.

1. Take turns with members of your family to choose a "Game Word" from the Game Bag at your table.

   The word will say "person," "animal," "transportation," "plant," or "occupation (job)."

   Put the word aside, not back in the Game Bag.

2. Use the Mulberry Street Game Board.

   Start at the beginning of the street, walk to Stop #1, select a Game Word, and write what you might see for the selected word.

   For example, if you picked the word "animal," you might write next to Stop #1, "I saw a cat chasing a dog!" Or, some other unusual sight.

3. Each time you or a family member stop at a new place on Mulberry Street, pick a Game Word and write down something that is stranger than the one before.

   Each sight along the way will get stranger and stranger.

4. After the last stop on Mulberry Street, choose your favorite sight and draw a picture of it on the back of your Mulberry Street Game Board.

5. Be prepared to share your list of strange sights and your picture with other families.

Mulberry Street Game Words (3-5)

Cut each set of five words into strips of paper, fold them, and place them in a Game Bag (e.g., a basket, bag, envelope, or other simple container) for each family. Make enough copies so that each family has a container with the five Game Words.

PERSON	PERSON
ANIMAL	ANIMAL
PLANT	PLANT
TRANSPORTATION	TRANSPORTATION
OCCUPATION (JOB)	OCCUPATION (JOB)
PERSON	PERSON
ANIMAL	ANIMAL
PLANT	PLANT
TRANSPORTATION	TRANSPORTATION
OCCUPATION (JOB)	OCCUPATION (JOB)

Mulberry Street Game Board (3-5)

Pick a word from the Game Bag and describe a strange sight at each stop on Mulberry Street.

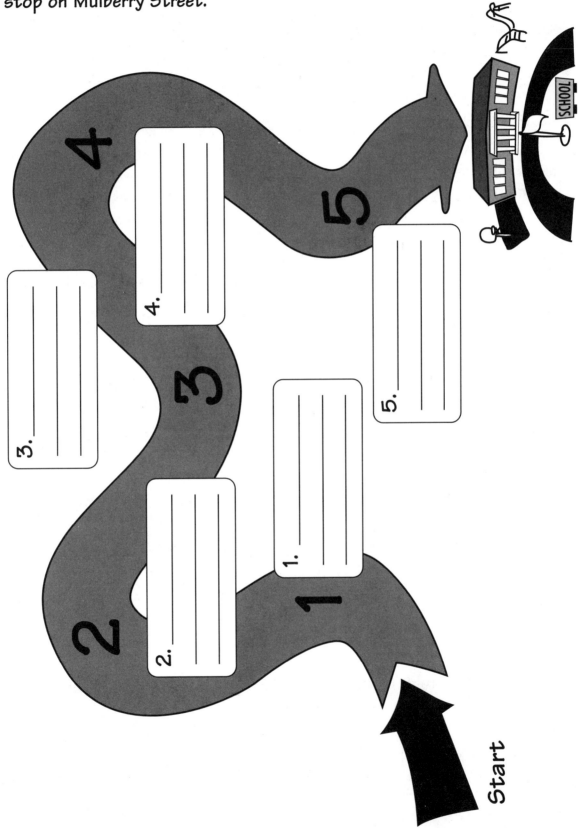

Classroom and Home Connection

Suggest that parents and children read *Green Eggs and Ham* by Dr. Seuss. After reading the story, discuss the book with such questions as:

- Did Sam want to try green eggs and ham?

- Where did he say he did *not* want to eat them?

- What did Sam think about green eggs and ham after he tried them?

Families and students can make green eggs at home with a few drops of food coloring. They may predict if the green eggs will taste different from regular eggs.

Provide a list of other books by Dr. Seuss that parents can read with their children in the primary and intermediate grades. Include a list of general questions that parents may ask to help their children share ideas about the books they read. These include:

- Tell me your favorite part of the book.

- Who did you think was the most interesting character?

- What was the best thing that happened?

- Did you enjoy this book? Why or why not?

The planning committee or Teacher-Leaders for *Dr. Seuss Family Night* may explore and/or share with parents a lively Web site with more ideas linked to the stories by Dr. Seuss: www.seussville.com.

Explore the Community

Encourage participants at *Dr. Seuss Family Night* to take a family trip to the zoo. They can learn about the animals and compare real animals at the zoo to Dr. Seuss's animals and those that they drew for the Zoo on the Wall.

Invite a zookeeper to come to class to talk about his/her work and responsibilities.

CHAPTER 9

Poetry Family Night
(April)

Poetry Family Night is synonymous with fun. Students and families will explore, write, and read different forms of poetry including nursery rhymes and song lyrics.

This event includes a whole-group activity writing acrostic poems, student presentations of their original poems, a poetry gallery to display students' work, and activities for families and students in the primary and intermediate grades.

Amazing Acrostic Poems
(Whole Group)

Students and their families will complete an acrostic poem together. At the end of the time period, the Teacher-Leader will ask for a few volunteer-poets to share their poems.

Materials

- 5 x 8 index cards (two Acrostic Poem Cards per family)
- Pencils, crayons, and/or markers
- *Family Page: Amazing Acrostic Poems*
- *Family Page: Poets Planning Page*

Skills Reinforced

- Building vocabulary
- Writing poems

POETRY GALLERY (STUDENT PRESENTATION)

Prior to *Poetry Family Night,* select one classroom or grade level for students to write original poems. Teachers may guide students to write different kinds of poems.

1. Different classes (or grade levels) may study different forms of poetry and write original poems (e.g., haiku, limerick, cinquain, ballad, diamante).

2. Display students' poems in a Poetry Gallery on the evening of *Poetry Family Night.* Include a definition or description of the type of poetry for parents and guests to see. The following Web site has definitions and examples of different types of poems: http://www.kathimitchell.com/poemtypes.html.

3. Choose one student from each participating grade level to explain one type of poem that they studied and to read an original poem for the audience on *Poetry Family Night.*

Amazing Acrostic Poems
(Whole Group)

Welcome to *Poetry Family Night*. We will begin our exploration of the wonderful world of poetry by writing an acrostic poem.

In an acrostic poem:

- A word, name, or phrase is written vertically on a paper.

- Each letter begins a new line of the poem.

- The poem must keep to the theme suggested by the word.

For example, an acrostic poem about reading might use the letters R-E-A-D to start each line, as shown here:

Reading makes me smart.

Enjoyable entertainment.

Adventure books are my favorite—

Don't skip a page or you will miss something!

As a family, write an acrostic poem together using the first name of one person in your family.

1. Choose the first name of a family member. It may be someone who is here or not. Write the name vertically down the left side of the Acrostic Poem Card.

2. Complete the Poets Planning Page to describe this person.

3. Use each letter of the person's first name to start a new line of poetry that describes him or her. Add an illustration if you have time.

4. Be prepared to share one of your poems with others.

Amazing Acrostic Poems (Whole Group)
Poets Planning Page

Use this page to list words and ideas that may be used in your acrostic poem.

PERSON IN MY FAMILY'S ACROSTIC POEM

First Name: _____

Likes and Dislikes: _____

_____

_____

_____

_____

Talents: _____

_____

_____

_____

_____

Other Interesting or Surprising Facts About This Person: _____

_____

_____

_____

_____

Well-Known Nursery Rhymes (K-2)

Humpty Dumpty

Humpty Dumpty sat on a wall.

Humpty Dumpty had a great fall.

All the king's horses and all the king's men

Couldn't put Humpty together again.

Hickory, Dickory, Dock

Hickory, dickory, dock,

The mouse ran up the clock.

The clock struck one,

The mouse ran down.

Hickory, dickory, dock.

Little Miss Muffet

Little Miss Muffet sat on a tuffet

Eating her curds and whey.

Along came a spider,

Who sat down beside her

And frightened Miss Muffet away.

Jack and Jill

Jack and Jill

Went up the hill

To fetch a pail of water.

Jack fell down

And broke his crown,

And Jill came tumbling after.

Jack, Be Nimble

Jack, be nimble.

Jack, be quick.

Jack, jump over

The candlestick.

For more nursery rhymes, see: www.zelo.com/family/nursery/

Call Me Mother Goose (K-2)

Materials

- Well-Known Nursery Rhymes page
- *Family Page: Call Me Mother Goose*
- Drawing paper
- Lined paper
- Pencils, crayons, and/or markers

Skills Reinforced

- Writing
- Increasing fluency

Activity

1. Give participants the *Well-Known Nursery Rhymes page.*
2. Conduct a choral group reading of some nursery rhymes, asking participants to listen for the rhythm of each rhyme.
3. Ask each family to work together and circle all of the rhyming words on the *Well-Known Nursery Rhymes page.*
4. Use the *Family Page: Call Me Mother Goose* to guide the students and families to work together to write and illustrate an original nursery rhyme modeled after the rhymes that were read aloud.
5. Select a few children to share their original nursery rhymes with the whole group.

Optional Discussion Questions

If time permits, ask the students and families:

- Why was it hard or easy for you to write an original nursery rhyme?
- What helped you to complete your rhyme?
- What is another of your favorite nursery rhymes? Can you lead us in saying it?

Optional Activity

Ask participants to give the group a clue that describes a well-known nursery rhyme character. Others will guess the character. Give one example, such as: "I am a little girl. Spiders frighten me." Participants will guess *Little Miss Muffet*.

*Teacher-Leaders may display and use nursery rhymes from diverse cultures. See, for example, the bilingual presentations and appealing illustrations in the following two books. Check the school or public library for other examples.: *Chinese Mother Goose Rhymes*, by Robert Wyndham, Paper Star Books, 1998. *Diez Deditos: Ten Little Fingers and Other Play Rhymes and Action Songs from Latin America*, Jose-Luis Orozco. Dutton, 1997.

Call Me Mother Goose (K-2)

Nursery rhymes are a great way to build children's reading and speaking skills and their love of poetry. We will share some well-known rhymes and write an original nursery rhyme.

1. Circle all of the rhyming words on the *Well-Known Nursery Rhymes* page.

2. Now, write an original rhyme with your family.

   Change only the rhyming words in this example.

   Little Miss _____

   Sat on a _____

   Eating her_____ and _____.

   Along came a_____,

   Who _____,

   And frightened Miss _____ _____.

3. Write a new nursery rhyme of your own, on lined paper. You may change the rhyming words of another poem that we read, or use one of the following prompts, or start with your own idea.

   FAMILIAR RHYME   NEW RHYME, STARTING...

   - Jack, be nimble, ⟶ (<u>Name</u>), be happy

   - Little Bo Peep has lost her sheep ⟶ Little (<u>someone</u>) lost his keys

   - Twinkle, twinkle, little star, ⟶ Glowing, glowing lovely moon

   - Hickory, dickory, dock ⟶ Slippery, whippery fish

   Remember: Use rhyming words and a good rhythm.

4. Use the drawing paper to add an illustration.

5. Be ready to share your New Nursery Rhyme with the group.

Musical Poetry (3-5)

Materials

- *Somewhere Over the Rainbow* and *We're Off to See the Wizard* on CD
- CD player
- Song lyrics from: http://thewizardofoz.warnerbros.com/movie/cmp/r-lyrics.html
- Pencils
- Lined paper
- Drawing paper
- Crayons and/or markers
- *Family Page: Musical Poetry*

Skills Reinforced

- Increasing fluency
- Building vocabulary

Activity

1. Before *Poetry Family Night*, secure a CD with the songs *Somewhere Over the Rainbow* and *We're Off to See the Wizard*, from the *Wizard of Oz*.

2. Play the songs for the students and families. Ask if they know what movie the songs are from. Ask questions such as:

   - Do you like the *Wizard of Oz*? Why or why not?

   - What pictures come to mind when you think about the movie?

3. Explain that songs from the *Wizard of Oz* and *all* songs are poetry set to music.

4. Give students and families copies of the lyrics for the two songs.

5. Review the terms "rhyme" and "alliteration."

6. Students and families will circle the rhyming words in *Somewhere Over the Rainbow* and examples of alliteration in *We're Off to See the Wizard*.

7. With their families, students will write a short, original poem on an imaginary land they would like to visit. They may illustrate the dream-like place on the back of the page or on drawing paper.

8. Gather families together to share their poems and talk over the optional discussion questions.

Optional Discussion Questions

- How are poetry and music related?
- How do you know that you like a song?

Musical Poetry (3-5)

Song lyrics are poems set to music. Many poets and songwriters use rhyming words and alliteration in their poems.

<u>Rhyming words</u> sound the same (e.g., <u>around</u> and <u>found</u>). Words usually rhyme at the end of sentences, but rhymes may occur anywhere.

<u>Alliteration</u> repeats the first consonant sound of words (e.g., <u>S</u>he <u>s</u>ells <u>s</u>ea <u>s</u>hells at the <u>s</u>eashore. And, see the <u>w</u> sound in <u>w</u>onderful <u>w</u>izard)

1. Let's read two poems that were set to music in very well-known songs.

   In *Somewhere Over the Rainbow,* circle the words that RHYME.

   In *We're Off to See the Wizard,* <u>underline examples of ALLITERATION</u>.

2. Now, it's your turn.

With your family, imagine a fantastic, wonderful place that you would like to visit. These questions will help you plan your poem. Fill in your ideas:

Where is your make-believe land? _____

What wonderful things will happen in this make-believe place?

_____

_____

Use your ideas above to help you write the poem. Give your poem a good title to fit the place you describe. Use drawing paper to illustrate the poem.

   TITLE: _____

   _____

   _____

   _____

   _____

Lyrics from: http://thewizardofoz.warnerbros.com/movie/cmp/r-lyrics.html

Classroom and Home Connection

In the activity Musical Poetry, students learned that songs are poems set to music. Encourage families to listen to the lyrics of some of their favorite songs at home. Students can listen for rhyming words, alliteration, and other poetic devices that they learned in class. Many song lyrics can be found at http://lyrics.com.

In class, review the activities from *Family Poetry Night* with all students, including those who were not able to attend the event. All students will enjoy Amazing Acrostic Poems, Call Me Mother Goose, or Musical Poetry.

Use different prompts than in the evening activities. For example, students may complete an acrostic poem using the name of the school, their favorite food, or a pet's name. Or, choose the lyrics of an age-appropriate popular song for the students to find rhymes and alliteration examples, with a theme to inspire them to write their own short poem.

Try putting some to music. Ask students to read their work aloud to a parent or family partner for homework.

Explore the Community

Invite a local songwriter, poet, or musician to talk with the whole school or a specific grade level that is writing poetry about the connections of poems, songs, and music.

CHAPTER 10

Biography Family Night
(May)

When they read biographies, children learn about famous people, positive character traits, and important and exciting contributions in all fields. Students may identify heroes and role models, learn about interesting careers, or glimpse history in the making.

Biography Family Night includes a whole-group activity and student presentation to identify famous people, and activities for families and students in the primary and intermediate grades to develop and share biographic information.

Three Clues
(Whole Group)

Families will think of three famous people or characters they know about in different categories, such as sports figures, authors and poets, musicians and singers, and cartoon characters. Those who wish to gather ideas may skim the collection of short biography books in the room. After writing down three facts or clues about these people, students and families will play "Three Clues." Teacher-Leaders should have one example on a chart to show families how to write their clues.

Materials

- Selection of biography books at different reading levels
- *Family Page: Three Clues*
- Paper and pencils

Skills Reinforced

- Summarizing
- Communicating ideas

WHO AM I? (STUDENT PRESENTATION)

Prior to *Biography Family Night*, select one classroom or grade level to read biographies about people in different fields (e.g., sports, music, movies, politics, history, medicine).

- Pretending they are the people they read about, students will write a short paragraph (*Who Am I?*) that provides clues about their lives and contributions to society.

- They also will draw a picture of the person they read about. All students' paragraphs and drawings will be posted on a **Wall of Fame** at *Biography Family Night*.

At *Biography Family Night*, five or six students will read their paragraphs for the audience to guess *Who Am I?* The presenters may wear a costume, a key article of clothing, or show an item linked to the famous person. These students' work should be posted *after* their presentations.

Three Clues
(Whole Group)

This evening, we will begin *Biography Family Night* with a game about famous people.

1. Work as a family to select three famous people from three different fields. They may be athletes, authors, actors, explorers, scientists, inventors, musicians, historians, or others. Name the people and their fields or talents. (You may check biographies in the room to look for ideas.)

2. Now, write three clues that describe why each person is famous, what they accomplished, where they grew up, or other facts that you know.

Three Famous People	Field/Talent	Three Clues
I._____	_____	a)_____
		b)_____
		c)_____
II._____	_____	a)_____
		b)_____
		c)_____
III._____	_____	a)_____
		b)_____
		c)_____

3. When you finish your list, play *Three Clues* with others at your table and nearby. Take turns with other families reading the clues and guessing the famous people who are described.

Bio-Mobile (K-2)

Materials

- Short picture book biographies (at least one per family)
- Wire or plastic coat hangers (one per family)
- 6 x 6 squares of white drawing paper or tagboard, hole punched at top center (at least three per child)
- Crayons and/or markers
- Pencils
- 12-inch pieces of string or yarn
- *Family Page: Bio-Mobile*

Skills Reinforced

- Summarizing
- Writing

Activity

1. Ask students and families to choose one short picture book biography to read as a family.

2. Guide students and families to select three facts about the person that they learned from the story. They will:

   - Write the *name* of the famous person and *one* fact on the back of each square for pictures.

   - Illustrate each fact, making three pictures.

   - String the three pictures and tie them to the coat hanger.

3. If some families finish early, they may read other biographies in the collection of books.

4. Invite two or three families to share their mobiles with the group. Display the completed mobiles in the classroom or hallway.

Optional Questions for Families to Discuss

- Why did you choose the biography you did?
- How is your life similar to or different from the person you read about?
- What would you ask the person you read about, if you met? Would you like to meet? Play with that person? Have dinner with that person? Why or why not?

Bio-Mobile (K-2)

Use the information from the book you read and the art supplies to make a bio-mobile about the famous person.

1. You will need these materials:

   - One coat hanger

   - Three pieces of white paper or poster board (hole-punched)

   - Three pieces of string

   - Crayons and/or markers

   - Pencils

2. Select one short biography to read with your family. Discuss some interesting facts and events that you learned about the person in your book.

3. On three drawing paper squares with holes punched, do the following:

   - On one side, write the name of the person and a sentence telling one important fact about the person's life and work.

   - On the other side, draw a picture illustrating the sentence.

   - You will have three facts and three pictures when you are done.

4. Use the strings to hang the three pictures from the bottom of the coat hanger to make a mobile.

5. If you finish your Bio-Mobile before the others, choose another biography to read.

6. When all families complete their Bio-Mobiles, we will share our creations and ideas.

Whose Face Is On Your Wheaties Box? (3-5)

Materials

- Short biography books (at least one per family)
- Empty cereal boxes (one per family)
- 11 x 17 drawing paper
- Pencils
- Crayons and/or markers
- Scissors
- Glue or tape
- *Family Page: Whose Face is on Your Wheaties Box?*

Skills Reinforced

- Thinking creatively
- Summarizing

Activity

1. Before *Biography Family Night*, ask students to bring in empty cereal boxes. Collect enough boxes for the number of families that sign up for the event. Have a few extra on hand, or other boxes of similar size.

2. Guide students and families to choose one biography book to read. If the books are long, families may skim the books to discover the main events of the person's life.

3. Students and families will discuss three to five facts about the person's life and work, based on what they learned from reading the book.

4. Using the *Family Page: Whose Face is on Your Wheaties Box?* and the art supplies that are provided, students and families will plan and make a picture for the front of the cereal box of the person they read about. They will give the cereal a name that fits that person's life or work.

5. Ask participants to share their boxes with the whole group, along with one or two facts they learned about the person.

Optional Discussion Questions

- Why did you select this person's biography?
- How are you similar to or different from this person?
- If you were grocery shopping, which cereal box that you saw would you buy?
- Why do you think companies like to put famous people on their products?

Whose Face Is On Your Wheaties Box? (3-5)

Many famous athletes have seen their faces on a box of Wheaties. Now, your family can highlight another famous person on a cereal box that you create.

1. Use the paper and art supplies that are provided. Cut the white paper to fit the front of your box. Then, set the paper and box aside for a while.

2. Select one short biography to read with your family. Discuss some interesting facts, events, and accomplishments that you learned about the person's life and work.

3. Think of a name for your cereal that describes your person's life and work.

   Write it in big letters at the top of the white paper, just like a real cereal box.

   For example, if you read a book about Dr. Martin Luther King, Jr., you might name your cereal "Dream-Os." A cereal for Queen Elizabeth might be called "Royal Crisps."

4. Now, draw a picture for the front of your cereal box that shows at least *one* important event or accomplishment of the person.

   It may be a portrait or the person in action.

   You may include key words about the person.

   Make your picture and words big, clear, and colorful so that someone will want to buy it and eat it!

5. Tape or glue the paper to the front of your cereal box.

   If you finish before other families, read another biography or discuss other facts about the person on your cereal box.

6. Be prepared to share the box you decorated with the whole group.

Classroom and Home Connection

Biography Family Night focused on the lives of famous individuals in history and modern times. Ask students who attended the event to share their new cereal boxes that they made and things they learned from the biographies they read.

Let all students know that there are important and interesting people in everyone's life. As a long-range homework assignment, ask students to interview a parent, grandparent, neighbor, senior citizen, store owner, or other adult who is important in their life. Then, use the answers to their questions to write a short biography of the individual, featuring their ideas, actions, and contributions to family and community.

Students may generate a list of interview questions in class, such as:

1. Where did you grow up?
2. Where did you go to school?
3. What is a funny or interesting story about your childhood?
4. When you were my age, what did you want to be when you grew up?
5. How did you choose your current profession?
6. What are your hobbies?
7. What are your future goals?
8. What advice would you give me about school and planning my future?

Students may add other questions for the person they select.

Share the life stories with a family member and in class.

Chapter Notes

Selected Web sites for booklists of children's biographies.

http://www.biography.com/bio4kids/index.jsp

http://www.sfgate.com/cgi-bin/article.cgi?f=/c/a/2006/11/19/RVGP7MEOEA1.DTL&type=books

http://www.carolhurst.com/booklists/biographies.html

http://nancykeane.com/rl/86.htm#Top

CHAPTER 11

Summer Reading Family Night
(June)

Summer is the time for beach trips, sleepovers, barbeques, and all kinds of fun. It also is a good time for students to read for pleasure and learn new things. *Summer Reading Family Night* engages students and families in planning enjoyable reading activities for the summer.

This event includes a whole group word game, student presentations on favorite reading activities completed throughout the school year, a primary grades activity creating reading puzzles, an intermediate grades activity creating story card games, and some ideas to take home for the summer.

Summer Reading Time
(Whole Group)

Family members will work together or with other families to find words in the phrase "Summer Reading." If they finish early, students and families can examine the collection of books in the room and discuss the kinds of books and magazines that they want to read over the summer.

Materials

- Display of children's favorite books, including Newbery Award and Caldecott Medal winners for the primary and intermediate grades.
- Pencils and paper
- *Family Page: Summer Reading*

Skills Reinforced

- Spelling
- Increasing vocabulary

CELEBRATING A YEAR OF READING! (STUDENT PRESENTATION)
Activity

1. Prior to *Summer Reading Family Night*, ask students from one classroom or grade level to select their favorite reading or writing activities that they completed during the year to display at the event. Students may select a book report, poem, short story, diorama, or other reading and related writing activity that they enjoyed.

2. During *Summer Reading Family Night*, all students' favorite reading and writing activities should be displayed around the room. Include with each product a display card with the student's name, date completed, and a sentence written by the student about why they enjoyed the activity.

3. Select up to five students to present their projects. They will describe the class lesson, the reading or writing activity that they enjoyed, and show their work that resulted from the lesson.

Summer Reading Time
(Whole Group)

Welcome to *Summer Reading Family Night.* Summer is full of surprises. Let's start tonight by finding words hidden in the phrase "Summer Reading."

Work as a family to make as many words as you can using ONLY the letters in SUMMER READING. Here is a hint: Look for "word families" such -as, -ar, -ad, -in, and -un. You may work with other families at your table.

S-U-M-M-E-R R-E-A-D-I-N-G

_____ _____ _____

_____ _____ _____

_____ _____ _____

_____ _____ _____

_____ _____ _____

Use the back of this page if you find more words!

When you complete the game of hidden words, explore the good books around the room with someone from your family.

Students: Which books and/or magazines do YOU want to read this summer? Make a list.

WHAT WILL YOU READ THIS SUMMER?

_____

_____

_____

_____

_____

Summer Story Puzzles (K-2)

Materials

- Summer picture books and other classic and favorite books for grades K-2
- 8½ x 11 white tagboard
- Pencils, crayons, and/or markers
- *Family Page: Summer Story Puzzles*
- A sample puzzle to show

Skills Reinforced

- Identifying main ideas
- Summarizing

Activity

1. Prior to *Summer Reading Family Night*, collect summer-themed picture books and other favorite books from the school library, public library, or other sources for students in grades K-2.

2. Invite each family to select one book to read and use for the activity.

3. Students will work with their families. On one side of a sturdy piece of tagboard, they will write the title of the book they read and one or two sentences about the **MAIN IDEA** of the story. Teacher-Leaders may pre-line the tagboard to make it easier for students and families to write their sentences.

4. Guide students to draw a big picture about the main idea of the story on the other side of the tagboard. They should fill the space with their picture. Have a sample picture that shows these steps.

5. When participants finish their picture, show them how to draw a few lines that divide the paper into six to 10 large sections. They may draw one or two wavy lines horizontally across the middle of the page and two or three wavy lines vertically spaced across the page. Then, they will cut across the lines to make their puzzle pieces.

   Use a sample to show how the puzzle lines are drawn and then cut.

6. Give students and families time to walk around the room to put together other families' puzzles, see the story pictures, and, on the other side, the sentences about the main ideas.

7. Bring the group together. Ask students which puzzles gave them ideas of good books to read over the summer. Give students and families age-specific book lists from the public library and other suggestions for enriching summer reading activities.

Summer Story Puzzles (K-2)

Create a picture puzzle that summarizes the main idea of a good book.

1. Choose a "summer" book or other good book in the room and read it with your family.

2. Talk about the main idea of the story.

3. Use the puzzle paper and art supplies that are provided.

   On one side of the paper, write the title of the book and one or two sentences that summarize the story's main ideas.

4. On the other side of the paper, draw a picture that illustrates one of the main ideas of the story.

   Make a nice big picture using the whole page and many different colors.

5. On the picture side, use a pencil to draw four or five wavy lines across and down the page to create six to 10 large puzzle pieces.

6. Cut the puzzle along the wavy lines to make your puzzle pieces.

7. Walk around the room to solve other families' puzzles and to learn about the books they read.

   On the back of this page, note the titles and authors of books you may want to read this summer.

Adapted from Bauer, K. & Drew, R. (1992) *Alternatives to worksheets.* Cypress, CA: CreativeTeaching Press, Inc.

Story Card Game (3-5)

MATERIALS

- Summer-themed picture and chapter books, and other classic and favorite books for grades 3-5
- 5 x 8 lined index cards (five per family)
- Pencils, crayons, and/or markers
- Paper clips or small binder clips (one per family)
- *Family Page: Story Card Game*

SKILLS REINFORCED

- Sequencing
- Summarizing

ACTIVITY

1. Prior to the *Summer Reading Family Night*, collect summer-themed picture books from the school library, public library, or other sources for students in grades 3-5. Collect books that have clear plots that will allow students to identify a sequence of events.

2. Invite each family to choose one book from the collection to read and use for the activity. If they select long books, students and families will read a chapter or portion of the book for the evening activity.

3. Give students and their families time to read (about 20 minutes), and then give a signal to stop reading. They will work together to discuss four important things that happened in the story or part they read.

4. Students will decorate one index card with the title, author, and picture of a character or main event. They will write one good sentence on each of four cards describing four main events that occurred in the story.

5. Then, they will mix up the cards and clip them together with a paper clip. The title card should go on top of the deck.

6. Students and families will visit other tables to play the card game and put the story cards in the order that they think they happened.

7. Ask two or three students to report on their books using their cards to tell the story.

8. Bring the group together before they leave. Ask students which card games suggested good books to read over the summer. Give students and families age-specific book lists from the public library and other ideas for enriching summer reading activities, as suggested at the end of this chapter.

Story Card Game (3-5)

Here is an easy-to-make game to play tonight. By playing the game with other families, you may discover books that you want to read this summer.

1. Read aloud the book that you selected with your family. You may take turns reading different pages or the student may do all of the reading. (If the book is long, select a chapter or section to read tonight.)

2. As a family, discuss four main events that happened in the story.

3. Use four index cards. Write one detailed sentence on each card to describe the four main events that you selected.

4. Use one more index card for the title, author, and picture of the main character or an event in the story.

5. Mix up your cards and paper-clip them together. Put the title card on top.

6. Test your story cards: Can you and your family partner put the cards in order for the story that you read?

7. Play the Story Card Game by moving from game to game. Visit other tables to put the cards in order showing what you think happened in the books that others read.

On the back of this page, note the titles and authors of books you may want to read this summer.

Classroom and Home Connection

Suggest home reading activities that students can complete with their families over the summer, using the take-home *Family Page* that follows. Activities include parents and children reading books for pleasure, keeping a summer journal, following directions to make a model or something to eat.

Teacher-Leaders can obtain age-specific and grade-specific book lists from the library or from one of the following Web sites.

California Department of Education
http://www.cde.ca.gov/ta/tg/sr/readinglist.asp
Click on "Search for a Reading List" for lists that can be printed by grade level.

Reading is Fundamental Book Lists
http://www.rif.org/educators/books/book_list_index.mspx

Also, see the Web site of the American Library Association, http://www.ala.org. Click on Awards and Book Awards for the past and present winners of the Caldecott (picture book) and Newbery (children's book) Medal winners.

Explore the Community

Encourage families to organize a summer book club with friends and neighbors. As a group, decide which book to read, when to meet, and fun activities to complete for each selection.

Attend summer reading activities at the local public library.

Invite a librarian from the public library to attend the *Summer Reading Family Night* and give all participants a library card and book lists for summer reading. This may be done during the first hour or as families leave for the evening.

Classroom and Home Connection

Reading and writing can be fun in the sun. Try these activities at home.

- <u>Write a summer journal</u>. Write daily events in a notebook. You may write about what you played, who played with you, or a trip you took. Give your opinions about a movie you saw, a book you read, or food you ate. You will enjoy reading your summer journal later in the year.

- <u>Make something</u>. Work with a parent to build, create, or cook something. You may build a model, learn to knit, cook a dessert, or follow other directions together.

- <u>Read for pleasure</u>. Set aside 15 minutes each night to read alone or read books aloud with your family. Parents may read books aloud to a young child or take turns reading aloud with an older child. Share what you are reading with your family and discuss why you like or dislike the books you read.

Explore the Community

Summer is a wonderful time to read for pleasure. Here are two ideas to have fun with reading.

- <u>Organize a book club with family, friends, and neighbors</u>. Decide as a group which books you will read, when you will meet, and how you will discuss each book. Choose books each participant can read on his/her own, a book that a parent reads aloud, and a book that a child reads to a parent or family member.

- <u>Ask the public librarian for recommendations of books to read and tips for starting or joining a book club</u>. Check into other library activities.

Forms for Planning Family Reading Nights

Family Reading Night Team Planning Guide

Theme: _____ **Date of Activity:** _____

Student Presentation: _____

Person in Charge	Assignment	Target Date	Notes	➥ Completed

Planning Check List

☐ Send home and collect invitations to families to register for event.

☐ Obtain dinner donations (e.g., food, paper products, drinks, etc.).

☐ Arrange child-care providers for very young children.

☐ Copy all handouts for the whole group, primary grades, and intermediate grades activities.

☐ Copy sign-in sheets and evaluation forms.

☐ Obtain paper, pencils, crayons, markers, and other supplies needed.

☐ Organize and train volunteers for specific responsibilities for the event.

☐ Purchase or collect prizes, raffles, and other incentives, as needed.

☐ _____

School Name and Logo

Date: _____

Dear Families,
You are invited to attend

Family Reading Night

Date: _____ Time: _____

Where: _____

Theme: _____

Student Presentation: _____

Please return the bottom of this page by _____.
Dinner will be served to all families who return this form.
We hope to see you at Family Reading Night!

Sincerely,
Teacher's Name
OR Family Reading Night Planning Committee

- -

Please return this to your child's homeroom teacher by _____.
(Date)

☐ YES, we will attend Family Reading Night on_____.
Number of people attending:_____

☐ NO, sorry we cannot attend Family Reading Night.

☐ NO, sorry we cannot attend, but please send a copy of the
Family Reading Night materials home with my child.

Name of parent _____

Name of child/children_____ Grade level(s) _____

Family Reading Night
Date:_____

Parents Name	Child's Name	Child's Grade Level

Homework Pass

For attending and participating in Family Reading Night

_____ is excused from

turning in homework that is due on _____.
(Date)

Homework Pass

For attending and participating in Family Reading Night

_____ is excused from

turning in homework that is due on _____.
(Date)

Homework Pass

For attending and participating in Family Reading Night

_____ is excused from

turning in homework that is due on _____.
(Date)

Family Reading Night

_____

School Name

_____

Date

Check the activities you attended tonight.

☐ Whole Group Activity
☐ Student Presentation
☐ Dinner
☐ Primary Grades Activity
☐ Intermediate Grades Activity

Please circle how much you agree:

	Strongly DISAGREE	Disagree	Agree	Strongly AGREE
I enjoyed this Family Reading Night.	SD	D	A	SA
The information was useful to me.	SD	D	A	SA

Please add your comments and suggestions.

What did you enjoy most?	What improvements do you suggest?

How might you follow up tonight's activities at home with your child?

THANK YOU VERY MUCH FOR YOUR IDEAS!